Oracle Certified Associate Java SE 8 Programmer – Practice Questions

- by Silviu Sosiade -

Introduction

Java certification is important for different reasons:

- Getting a Java certification is a common way to demonstrate that a job candidate has the skills to understand and write code using Java programming language.

- A Java certification can often save the hassle of dealing with interview questions like: "How do write a simple program in Java?" or "How do you compile a program in Java?. At a first glance this does not seem much. But a reputable certification can do half of the job required in passing the interview with flying colours.

- A Java certification can help a fresh graduate to compensate to some extent for the lack of experience in Java programming offering increased chances in getting their first programmer job.

- Also for a non-Java programmer looking for a career change, getting a certification can facilitate this transition.

There are many cases of Java programmers with some experience in this area choosing to obtain certifications in order to prove their level of competence.

Oracle Java certifications (formerly known as "Sun Java Certifications") have probably the best reputation in this area. Such certifications are also difficult to obtain. Oracle University does not disclose any statistics regarding various exams passing rates. But the stories of those who have passed these tests support the idea that without investing sufficient time and effort these exams are difficult to pass.

Oracle offers a full suite of exams for different levels of expertise in Java (you can inspect http://education.oracle.com for all the trainings and certifications available). However for beginners the most popular are:

- Java Programmer I (or "Oracle Certified Associate")

- Java Programmer II (or "Oracle Certified Professional")

Conducting an examination consists of answering a number of questions in a given time frame. If you get more questions right than a certain percentage then - congratulations! - you have passed the exam.

For example, "Programmer Java SE7 I" contains 70 questions, the response time is 120 minutes and the passing score is 63%. At the beginning of 2015, the exam "SE8 Java Programmer I" was introduced. It contains 77 questions, the response time is 120 minutes and the passing score is 65%.

A common comment of those who attended this examination is the time is very tight or not enough. Because of this reason the exam preparation requires some (significant) practice in answering the examination type of questions in order to ensure success in passing the exam.

This is the main purpose of this book: to offer a number of questions similar to those seen during examination. The book is intended to help the candidate practice and get some experience in answering these type of exam questions.

The questions are selected in accordance with the examination syllabus for "Oracle Certified Associate" and cover the following topics:

- Structure of the Java software; how to compile and execute it

- Use Java programming language constructs and basic data types

- Use decision and looping constructs in order to control the flow schedule

- Understand basic object oriented concepts such as inheritance, encapsulation, and abstraction. Classes and Interfaces

- Use and manipulate object references

- Error handling code. Java Exceptions

- Understand lambda functions

The questions are in random order to simulate how they appear during the examination.

The book is split into two sections:

1) **Questions Only** - the answers are not visible at the end of each question, facilitating the completion of a number of questions in order to measure the time spent in answering the questions.

2) **Questions and Answers** – where the answers and explanations are present at the end of every question. You can use this section of the book to check your answers. Or go through the list of questions one by one and check your response for every question you answered.

There are questions with one answer or multiple answers and this is clearly indicated by each question.

The Java code in each question is assumed to be contained within the same file unless stated otherwise.

This books assumes that the candidate has some basic understanding of Java language and concepts before starting practicing for the exam. The purpose of this book is not to substitute a Java course but to train the candidate in answering questions. Therefore it is recommended to consult a Java course beforehand.

All the answers provide explanations, indicating why options are correct or incorrect. Although I tried to keep these explanations short and clear, you might find some answers are quite sketchy. If this is the case and you feel you need more information about a certain area, then you should use additional resources (online resources or a good Java book).

Do not forget to rate the speed you answer the questions. Before you leave for the exam centre you must have enough confidence that you can answer at least 70-80 such questions in approximately 2 hours.

The preparation for the exam could be a lot more time consuming that initially thought. So do not put yourself under unnecessary pressure by scheduling the exam too early.

I strongly advise you to try the examples from this book using a Java compiler or a Java IDE. Such practice is essential in getting the ability of answering some questions quickly and correctly. I personally used Eclipse for preparing this book and I have always found this tool extremely powerful. And it is also free to download and straightforward to install. But any Java IDE you are comfortable with or intend to explore should serve this purpose as well.

Finally I would like to thank you for choosing this book. I hope it will be a valuable companion in your preparation for passing your exam.

Good luck!

Silviu Sosiade

Questions Only

Question 1) Which of the following are correct? Choose all that apply.

a.
```
import java.lang.*;
class Test {
}
```

b.
```
import java.lang.*;
package com.ocjpa.mockexams;
class Test {
}
```

c.
```
package com.ocjpa.mockexams;
package com.ocjpa.learning;
import java.util.*;
public class Test {
}
```

d.
```
package com.ocjpa.mockexams;
import java.util.ArrayList;
import java.util.*;
public class Test {
}
```

e.
```
package com.ocjpa.mockexams.*;
public class Test {
}
```

Question 2) What is the result of evaluating 2^2 expression? Select one correct answer.

a. 0

b. 2

c. 4

d. none of the above

Question 3) Which of the following represent correct method declarations? Choose all that apply.

```
a. int foo(int a,b)
```

```
b. int foo(int a, int b)
```

```
c. int foo(int a=0, int b)
```

```
d. int foo(int a, int b=0)
```

```
e. int foo(int a=0, int b=0)
```

```
f. int foo(int... a)
```

Question 4) Given the following Java classes select the correct statements. Choose all that apply.

```
package com.ocjpa.mockexams;
class Base {
    private int private_data;
    protected int protected_data;
    public int public_data;
```

```
    int data;
    private void doPrivateMethod() {}
    protected void doProtectedMethod() {}
    public void doPublicMethod() {}
    final void doFinalMethod() {}
}
class Foo extends Base {
}
```

a. "private_data" is visible in class Foo

b. "protected_data" is visible in in class Foo

c. "public_data" is visible in class Foo

d. "data" is visible in class Foo

e. "doPrivateMethod()" is visible in class Foo

f. "doProtectedMethod()" is visible in class Foo

g. "doPublicMethod()" is visible in class Foo

h. "doFinalMethod()" is visible in class Foo

Question 5) Which of the following constructs are incorrect? Select one answer.

a.
```
public class Circle {
    public double getCircleArea(double radius) {
        return Math.PI*radius*radius;
    }
}
```

b.
```
import static java.lang.Math.PI;
public class Circle {
    public double getCircleArea(double radius) {
        return PI*radius*radius;
    }
}
```

c.
```
import static java.lang.Math.*;
public class Circle {
    public double getCircleArea(double radius) {
        return PI*radius*radius;
    }
}
```

d.
```
import java.lang.Math.*;
public class Circle {
    public double getCircleArea(double radius) {
        return PI*radius*radius;
    }
}
```

Question 6) What is the number of bytes used to represent a Java primitive type int? Select one correct answer.

a. it is dependent on the Java compiler

b. it is dependent on the operating system

c. 2

d. 4

e. 8

10

f. none of the above

Question 7) What is the output of the following Java program? Select one answer.

```
public class MyClass {
    public static void main(String[] args) {
            int sel = 0;
            switch(sel) {
                case 0: System.out.print(0);
                case 1: System.out.print(1); break;
                case 2: System.out.print(2);
                case 3: System.out.print(3); break;
                default: System.out.print(4);
            }
    }
}
```

a. 0

b. 01

c .012

d. 0123

e. 01234

f. none of the above

Question 8) Given the following Java program select the correct answer.

```
class MyClass {
```

```
void swap(int a, int b) {
    int tmp;
    tmp = a;
    a = b;
    b = tmp;
}
public static void main(String[] args){
    int a=1, b=2, c=3;
    swap(a,b);
    swap(b,c);
    System.out.println(a + " " + b + " " +
c);
}
}
```

a. it will produce a compilation error

b. it will display: 1 2 3

c. it will display: 2 3 1

d. it will display: 2 1 3

Question 9) What is the output of the following Java program? Select one correct answer.

```
class Base {
    int data = 1;
    int getData() {
        return data;
    }
}
class Derived extends Base {
    int data = 2;
}
class MyClass {
```

```
public static void main(String[] args)
{
        Base base = new Base();
        Derived derived = new Derived();
        System.out.print(base.getData());
        System.out.println(derived.getData());
}
}
```

a. 11

b. 12

c. 22

d. compilation error because "data" from class Base is duplicated in class Derived.

Question 10) Which of the following statements is true? Select one correct answer.

a. all the errors and exceptions extend the class java.lang.Throwable

b. Java programs must handle all the exceptions

c. "Error" and "RuntimeException" means the same thing and can be used interchangeably

d. user defined exceptions can only be checked exceptions

Question 11) What is the output of the following Java program? Select one correct answer.

```
import static java.lang.Math.*;
public class Circle {
    public double getCircleArea(double radius) {
        return PI*radius*radius;
    }
    public static void main(String[] args){
        System.out.println(getCircleArea(10));
    }
}
```

a. the program will fail to compile

b. it will print 314.1592653589793

c. it will compile correctly but will give an error at runtime

d. it will print 3.141592653589793

Question 12) What is the output of the following Java program? Select one correct answer.

```
public class MyClass {
    public static void main(String[] args) {
        int sel = 0;
        switch(sel) {
            case 0: System.out.print(0);
            case 1: System.out.print(1);
            case 2: System.out.print(2);
            case 3: System.out.print(3);
            default: System.out.print(4);
        }
    }
}
```

a. 0

b. 0123

c. 01234

d. none of the above

Question 13) What happens when the following Java code is compiled and run? Select one correct answer.

```
package com.ocjpa.mockexams;
public class TestMultipleMain {
    public static void main(String args) {
        System.out.println("First main method");
    }
    public static void main(String[] args) {
        System.out.println("Second main
method");
    }
}
```

a. the program will fail to compile

b. the program will print "First main method" followed by "Second main method"

c. the program will print "First main method"

d. the program will print "Second main method"

e. the program will produce an error at runtime

f. none of the above

Question 14) What is the range of values that can be specified for Java primitive type `int`? Select one correct answer.

a. this is compiler dependent

b. this is operating system dependent

c. -2^{31} to $2^{31} - 1$

d. any integer value can be used

Question 15) What is the output the following program? Select one correct answer.

```java
public class MyClass {
    public static void main(String[] args) {
        int sel = 0;
        switch(sel) {
            case "0": System.out.print(0);
            case "1": System.out.print(1);
            break;
            case "2": System.out.print(2);
            case "3": System.out.print(3);
            break;
            default: System.out.print(4);
        }
    }
}
```

a. 0

b. 01

c. 4

d. the program will display nothing

e. compilation error

Question 16) Given the following statements select all the correct answers?

a. for a "while" loop the exit condition is evaluated before entering the loop

b. the code inside the "do – while" loop is executed at least once

c. the code inside the "while" loop is executed at least once

d. "do – while" and "while" can only define a single line of code to execute

Question 17) What is the output when the following code is compiled and run? Select one correct answer.

```
class classA{
    private int memberClassA;
    public void setNumber(int number){
        memberClassA = number;
    }
}
public class Test{
    public static void main(String[] args) {
        classA  objA = new classA();
        objA.memberClassA = 10;
        System.out.println(objA.memberClassA);
        objA.setNumber(20);
        System.out.println(objA.memberClassA);
    }
}
```

a. It will fail to compile

b. It will compile but fail to execute

c. It will print 10 twice

d. It will print 10 followed by 20

Question 18) Given the following Java program, select the correct answer.

```
class MyClass {
      static void swap(int var1, int var2) {
          int tmp;
          tmp = var1;
          var1 = var2;
          var2 = tmp;
      }
      public static void main(String[] args){
          int a=1, b=2, c=3;
          swap(a,b);
          swap(b,c);
          System.out.println(a + " " + b + " " +
c);
      }
}
```

a. it will produce a compilation error

b. it will display: 1 2 3

c. it will display: 2 3 1

d. it will display: 2 1 3

Question 19) Assuming the classes below are in the same package, which of the following statements is correct? Select one correct answer.

```
class Base {
    private int data;
    void setData(int data) {
        this.data = data;
    }
    int getData() {
        return this.data;
    }
}
class Derived extends Base {
    void setData(int data) {      // 1
        super.setData(data);      // 2
    }
    int getData( {                // 3
        return super.getData();   // 4
    }
}
```

a. error at //1 and //2 because the methods in derived class have the same name as in the base class

b. error at //2 because the "data" passed as parameter clashes with the object field "data"

c. error at //2 and //4 because the syntax used to call a base class method is incorrect

d. error at //2 and //4 because "setData" and "getData" are not marked as "public" and they are not accessible in class Derived

e. error at //2 and //4 because the Derived class is ultimately trying to access the private object field "data" of the Base class

f. none of the above

Question 20) What is the output of the following Java program? Select one correct answer.

```
public class MyClass {
        int data = 0;
        public void Method3() throws Exception {
            throw new Exception();
        }
        public void Method2() throws Exception {
            Method3();
            data++;
        }
        public void Method1() {
            try {
                data++;
                Method2();
                data++;
            }
            catch (Exception e) {
                data++;
            }
            finally {
                data++;
            }
            System.out.println(data);
        }
        public static void main(String args[]) {
            new MyClass().Method1();
        }
}
```

a. 0

b. 1

c. 2

d. 3

e. 4

f. 5

Question 21) What is the output of the following code? Select one correct answer.

```
class classA {
    int memberClassA = 20;
    public void setNumber(int memberClassA){
        memberClassA = memberClassA;
    }
    public int getNumber(){
        return memberClassA;
    }
}
public class TestMultipleMain {
    public static void main(String[] args) {
        classA  objA = new classA();
        objA.setNumber(30);
        System.out.println(objA.getNumber());
    }
}
```

a. the program will not compile

b. runtime exception

c. it will print 20

d. it will print 30

e. no output is produced

Question 22) What will the following program print when trying to compiled and execute it? Select one correct answer.

```
public class MyClass {
    public static void main(String args[]) {
    int i = 1;
    System.out.println(++i+i++);
    }
}
```

a. compilation error

b. 1

c. 3

d. 4

e. 5

Question 23) Given the following statements select all the correct answers.

a. when a new object is created using the new keyword, memory is allocated for the new instance of the class

b. the default constructor is always called prior to returning the reference to the new object

c. a constructor is called to perform the initialization of the object

d. a reference to the object is returned

Question 24) Which of the following are correct declarations of a top level Java class? Select all that apply.

a. public class MyClass{}

b. public static class MyClass{}

c. private class MyClass{}

d. class MyClass{}

e. protected class MyClass{}

Question 25) Why does the following class break the principles of data encapsulation? Select one correct answer.

```
public class Circle {
    public float radius = 5;
    static final double PI = 3.14;
    void setRadius(double radius) {
        this.radius = radius;
    }
    double getRadius() {
        return this.radius;
    }
}
```

a. there are no get/set methods for PI

b. "radius" is declared as "public"

c. PI has the "static" modifier

d. PI is "final" so it cannot longer be modified

23

e. the class has no constructor

f. "radius" is not initialized in any constructor

Question 26) Given the following statements, select one correct answer.

```
class Base {
    void doMethodA() {
        System.out.println("Method A in Base");
    }
    void doMethodB() {                    // 1
        System.out.println("Method B in Base");
    }
}
class Derived extends Base {
    void doMethodA() {
        System.out.println("Method A in
Derived");
    }
    int doMethodB() {                     // 2
        System.out.println("Method B in
Derived");
        return 0;
    }
}
class MyClass {
    public static void main(String[] args)
    {
        Derived d = new Derived();
        d.doMethodA();
        d.doMethodB();
    }
}
```

a. the program will print "Method A in Base" followed by "Method B in Base"

b. the program will print "Method A in Base" followed by "Method B in Base"

c. the program will print "Method A in Base" followed by "Method B in Derived"

d. compilation error at line // 2

Question 27) Given the following Java program:

```
public class CmdLineParams {
    public static void main(String[] args) {
        System.out.print(args.length+" ");//
Line 1
        System.out.print(args[0]+" ");// Line 2
        System.out.print(args[1]+" ");// Line 3
    }
}
```

What is the output if the program is run with the following command:

java CmdLineParams 12 3

Select one correct answer.

a. 3 12 3

b. 3 CmdLineParams 12

c. 3 1 2

d. 2 12 3

e. 2 CmdLineParams 12 3

25

Question 28) Which of the following statements are true? Choose all that apply.

a. "static variables" are also known as "class variables"

b. "instance variables" are also known as "static fields"

c. static members can access non static methods and variables

d. static members can be accessed even if no instances of the class are created

Question 29) Which of the following are correct array declarations in Java? Select all that apply.

```
a.  int a[5][];

b.  int a[][];

c.  int[5][] a;

d.  int[5][5] a;

e.  int a[5][5];

f.  int[][] a;

g.  int[]a[];
```

Question 30) Given the following Java program, select all the correct answers.

```
class DoWhileDemo {
    public static void main(String[] args) {
        int count = 0;
        do {
            System.out.print(count);
            count++;
            while(count > 0) {
                --count;
                System.out.print(count);
            }
        } while (count < 11);
        System.out.println(count);
    }
}
```

a. the program will print 10 an infinite number of times

b. the program will print 0 an infinite number of times

c. at the end of the program the value of count is 12

d. at the end of the program the value of count is 11

Question 31) Given the following class, select the all the correct answers.

```
class MyJavaClass {
    private String field1;
    private String field2;
    private int numericField;
    MyJavaClass(String field1) {         // 1
        this.field1 = field1;
    }
    MyJavaClass(String field2) {         // 2
        this.field2 = field2;
    }
```

```
    MyJavaClass(String f1, String f2) {   // 3
            this.field1 = f1;
            this.field2 = f2;
    }
    MyJavaClass(String f1, String f2,int num) {
// 4
            this.numericField = num;
            this(f1, f2);                      // 5
    }
    MyJavaClass(String f1,  int num, String f2) {
// 6
        this.numericField = num;
        this.field1 = f1;
        this.field2 = f2;
    }
}
```

a. constructors cannot be overloaded in Java

b. overloaded constructors at line //1 and line //2 are not correct as "field1" and "field2" passed as parameters have the same name as the class fields

c. overloaded constructors at line //1 and line //2 are not correct as they have the same signature

d. a constructor cannot be invoked using the statement in line //5

e. the constructors defined at lines //4 and //6 are identical

Question 32) Which of the following statements are true regarding the @Override annotation? Select one correct answer.

a. it is just some note in the code reading a method that we want to override and it has no effect on compilation

b. it controls whether or not a particular method is overloaded

c. it forces the compiler to check that method overrides a method from the base class

d. it allows to override a method from the base class but using a different name

Question 33) What is the output of the following Java program assuming that the file "test.txt" does not exist? Select one correct answer.

```java
import java.io.File;
import java.io.FileNotFoundException;
import java.io.FileReader;
import java.io.IOException;
class MyFileException extends
FileNotFoundException {}
public class MyClass {
    public void Method() {
        try {
            File file = new File("test.txt");
            FileReader fileReader = new
FileReader(file); // 1
        }
        catch (MyFileException e) {
            System.out.println("I was here 1");
        }
        catch (IOException e) {
            System.out.println("I was here 2");
        }
        catch (Exception e) {
            System.out.println("I was here 3");
        }
        finally {
            System.out.println("I was here 4");
        }
```

```
        }
    public static void main(String args[]) {
        new MyClass().Method();
    }
}
```

a. "I was here 1"

b. "I was here 2"

c. "I was here 3"

d. "I was here 4"

e. "I was here 1" **followed by** "I was here 4"

f. "I was here 2" **followed by** "I was here 4"

g. "I was here 3" **followed by** "I was here 4"

Question 34) What is the output of the following code? Select one correct answer.

```
public class TestLocalVar {
    private String var = "Hello World";
    public void printVar(){
        String var = "Hello everyone";    //1
        System.out.println(var);          //2
    }
    public static void main(String[] args){
        TestLocalVar obj = new TestLocalVar();
        obj.printVar();
    }
}
```

a. compilation error in line 1 as there is already a variable with the same name

b. compilation error in line 2 as the code is trying to access a private member

c. "Hello World"

d. "Hello everyone"

Question 35) What is the output of the following program? Select one correct answer.

```
public class MyClass {
    public static void main(String args[]) {
        int i = 1, r;
        r = r ^ i++;
        System.out.println(r);
    }
}
```

a.compilation error

b. 0

c. 1

d. 2

e. undefined

Question 36) Which of the following are not valid lambda function definitions in Java? Select one answer.

a. () -> System.out.println(this)

31

b. `(String str) -> System.out.println(str)`

c. `str -> System.out.println(str)`

d. `(String s1, String s2) -> { return s2.length() - s1.length(); }`

e. `(s1, s2) -> s2.length() - s1.length()`

f. `() -> 8`

g. `() -> {9}`

h. `a -> System.out.println(str)`

i. `a,b -> a-b`

Question 37) What is the output of the following code? Select one correct answer.

```java
public class Car {
    private void accelerate() {
        System.out.println("Car accelerating");
    }
    private void break() {
        System.out.println("Car breaking");
    }
    public void control(boolean faster) {
        if (faster == true)
            accelerate();
        else
        break();
    }
    public static void main(String[] args){
        Car car = new Car();
        car.control(false);
```

```
        }
}
```

a. the code fails to compile

b. Car accelerating

c. Car breaking

d. no output

e. none of the above

Question 38) What is the output of the following program? Select one correct answer.

```
public class MyClass {
    public static void main(String args[]) {
    int i = 2, r = 1;
    r = r++ ^ i++;
    System.out.println(r);
    }
}
```

a. compilation error

b. 0

c. 1

d. 2

e. 3

f. 4

Question 39) Which command line is the correct way of compiling a Java class? Select one correct answer.

a. java Test.java

b. java Test

c. javac Test.class

d. javac Test

e. javac Test.java

Question 40) Which of the following are not Java primitive types? Select all that apply.

a. byte

b. short

c. integer

d. long

e. float

f. double

g. bool

h. char

Question 41) What is the output of the following program?

34

Select one correct answer.

```
public class MyClass {
    public static void main(String args[]) {
        int i = 10;
        if (i++ % 10)
        {
            System.out.println("True");
        }
        else
        {
            System.out.println("False");
        }
    }
}
```

a. compilation error

b. "True"

c. "False"

d. runtime exception

Question 42) What is wrong with the following array initialization? Select one correct answer.

```
class ArrayTest {
    public static void main(String[] args) {
        // declares an array of integers
        int[] arr;
        arr[0] = 1;
        arr[1] = 2;
        arr[2] = 3;
        arr[3] = 4;
    }
```

```
}
```

a. `arr` length is not specified in the array variable declaration

b. `arr` is only declared but never created

c. the correct syntax for an array declaration is "`int arr[];`", not "`int[] arr;`"

d. none of the above

Question 43) Which of the following constructs are infinite "`while`" loops? Choose all that apply.

a. `while(1) {};`

b. `while(true);`

c. `while(true) {};`

d. `while(10 % 2);`

e. `while(1==1){}`

f. `while(1 & 1);`

g. `while(1 && 1);`

Question 44) What happens when the following code is compiled and run? Select one correct answer.

```
public class TestClass {
    private static String hello = "Hello world";
    public static void main(String args){
```

```
        System.out.println(hello.length());
    }
}
```

a. compilation error

b. runtime error

c. it will display: 11

d. it will display: 12

e. code is executed but no output is produced

Question 45) Given the code below, what is the reference count for the object created at line // 1 when the program execution is reaching the line System.out.println("Here")? Select one correct answer.

```
class MyClass {
    public int val = 5;
    void displayVal(MyClass c) {
        System.out.println(c.val);
        System.out.println("Here");  // <- what
is the reference count for "obj" here?
    }
    public static void main(String[] args){
        MyClass obj = new MyClass(); // 1
        obj.displayVal(obj);
    }
}
```

a. 0

b. 1

c. 2

d. cannot be determined

Question 46) Which of the following statements are true? Choose all that apply.

```
class Base {
    public int data = 0;

    void setData(int data) {
        this.data = data;
    }
}
class Derived extends Base {
    final void setData(int data) {   // 1
        this.data = data;            // 2
    }
}
```

a. the code above will produce no compilation errors

b. the compiler will complain at line //1 because it tries to override a final method

c. the compiler will complain at line //2 because "data" is not a member of class "Derived"

d. class "Derived" cannot be inherited because it contains a final method

e. class "Derived" cannot be instantiated because it contains a final method

f. method "setData" cannot be overridden in any classes inherited from class "Derived"

38

Question 47) Which of the following operators is not an arithmetic operator? Select one correct answer.

a. +

b. -

c. &

d. *

e. /

f. %

Question 48) What is the output of the following Java program assuming that the file "data.txt" does not exist in the current folder? Select one correct answer.

```
import java.io.*;
public class MyClass {
    public void MyMethod() {
        try {
            FileInputStream input = new
FileInputStream("data.txt");
            input.close();
        }
        catch (IOException e) {
                System.out.println("I was
here 1");
        }
        catch(Exception e) {
            System.out.println("I was here 2");
        }
```

```
    }
    public static void main(String args[]) {
        new MyClass().MyMethod();
    }
}
```

a. it displays "I was here 1"

b. it displays "I was here 2"

c. it displays "I was here 1" followed by "I was here 2"

d. nothing will be displayed

Question 49)   What happens when the following code is compiled and run? Select one correct answer.

```
public class TestClass {
    private static String hello = "Hello world";
    public static void main(String... params){
        System.out.println(hello.length());
    }
}
```

a. compilation error

b. runtime error

c. it will display: 11

d. it will display: 12

e. code is executed but no output is produced

Question 50) Which of the following are not valid Java

operators? Choose all that apply.

a. %

b. <>

c. <<

d. $

e. ++

f. #

g. ~

h. instanceof

Question 51) What will be the output of the following program? Select one correct answer.

```
class MyClass {
    public int val = 5;
    void change(int a, MyClass c) {
        c.val = 10;
        a = 20;
    }
    public static void main(String[] args)
    {
        MyClass obj = new MyClass();
        obj.change(obj.val, obj);
        System.out.println(obj.val);
    }
}
```

a. Error

b. 5

c. 10

d. 20

Question 52) Given the following program, select the correct statements. Select one answer.

```
package packageA;
class ClassA {
    public String memberA;
}
package packageB;
import packageA.ClassA;
public class ClassB{
}
```

a. it will print null

b. it will not print anything as memberA was not initialised

c. it will not compile

d. it will compile but it will throw an exception at runtime

Question 53) Which of the following represent incorrect variable initializations in Java. Choose all that apply.

```
a.  int val = 25;

b.  int val = 025;

c.  int val = a10;
```

42

```
d. int val = 0x27;

e. int val = 0b10010;

f. long longer = 999_99_9999L;

g. int val = 27hex;
```

Question 54) What is the output of the following program? Select one answer.

```
public class MyClass {
    public static void main(String args[]) {
        int a = 3, b = 2, c = 0;
        int r;
        r = ++a + 1 * b << 4 - 3*c;
        System.out.println(r);
    }
}
```

a. 0

b. 96

c. 100

d. the code will fail to compile

Question 55) Which of the following represent correct array initializations? Choose all that apply.

```
a.   int[] arr = { 1, 2, 3, 4};

b.   int[4] arr = { 1, 2, 3, 4};
```

```
c.    int[] arr = [ 1, 2, 3, 4];

d.    int[] arr = { {1}, {2}, {3}, {4}};

e.    int[][] arr = { {1}, {2}, {3}, {4}};
```

Question 56) Which of the following represents a correct way of writing an infinite "do-while" loop? Choose all that apply.

```
a. do {} while(1);

b. do {} while(true);

c. do {} while(10 % 2);

d. do {} while(1==1);

e. do {} while(1 & 1);

f. do {} while(1 && 1);
```

Question 57) Which statements are true regarding the following Java class? Select one correct answer.

```
public class Foo {
      private int a,b,c;
      Foo (int a, int b, int c) {
            this.a = a;
            this.b = b;
            this.c = c;
      }
      Foo (int c, int d) {        // 1
            this(c,d,1);          // 2
      }
      Foo (int a, int b) {        // 3
```

44

```
                this.a = a;
                this.b = b;
                this.c = 1;
        }
}
```

a. the construct this(c, d, 1) is not valid

b. the second and the constructors are duplicated

c. the code will not compile as the default constructor is missing

d. the code will not generate any compilation errors

Question 58) What is the output of the following program? Select one correct answer.

```
class Base {
    public int data = 0;
    void setData(int data) {
        System.out.println("Base class called");
        this.data = data;
    }
}
class Derived extends Base {
    boolean setData(int newData) {
        System.out.println("Derived class
called");
        this.data = newData;
        return true;
    }
}
class MyClass {
    public static void main(String[] args)
    {
        Derived obj = new Derived();
```

```
        obj.setData(5);
    }
}
```

a. the code will fail to compile because "setData" of the Derived class does not return the same type as "setData" of the Base class

b. will display "Base class called"

c. will display "Derived class called"

d. will display "Derived class called" followed by "Base class called"

Question 59) What is the output of the following program? Select one correct answer.

```
class AException extends Exception {}
class BException extends AException {}
class CException extends BException {}

public class MyClass {
    public void Method() {
        try {
            throw new CException();
        }
        catch(BException e) {          // 1
            System.out.println("Caught
BException");
        }
        catch(Exception e) {           // 2
            System.out.println("Caught
Exception");
        }
        catch(CException e) {
```

```
            System.out.println("Caught
CException");   // 3
        }
    }
    public static void main(String args[]) {
        new MyClass().Method();
    }
}
```

a. it will display "Caught BException"

b. it will display "Caught Exception"

c. it will display "Caught CException"

d. the code will fail to compile

Question 60) We want the instance variable myTest to be accessible only to classes and interfaces defined in the same package. Which of the following declarations should be used? Select one correct answer.

a. private String myTest;

b. protected String myTest;

c. default String myTest;

d. String myTest;

e. public String myTest;

Question 61) What is the output of the following program? Select one correct answer.

47

```
public class MyClass {
    public static void main(String args[]) {
        int var = 10;
        System.out.print(var++);
        System.out.println(++var);
    }
}
```

a. 1012

b. 1011

c. 1112

d. 1111

Question 62) Which statements are true regarding the following Java class? Choose all that apply.

```
public class MyClass {
    private int key;
    public int getKey () {                  // 1
                return (int) key;
    }
    public float getKey () {                // 2
                return (float) key;
    }
    public float getKey (float salt) {  // 3
                return (float) key;
    }
}
```

a. method "getKey()" at //1 is correctly overloaded at //2

b. method "getKey()" at //2 is correctly overloaded at //3

c. the compiler will determine which "getKey()" method to use

d. the compiler will flag both line //1 and line //2 indicating that the two methods are duplicated.

Question 63) Which statements are true regarding the following Java program? Select one correct answer.

```
public class Test {
    static int count;
    public void printCount(){
        System.out.print(count+ " ");
        count ++;
    }
    public static void main(String[] args){
        Test myTest = new Test();
        myTest.printCount();
        Test yourTest = new Test();
        yourTest.printCount();
    }
}
```

a. it will not compile as a non static method cannot access static members

b. it will not compile because count is not initialized and the compiler only assigns default values to non initialized non static members

c. it will print 0 0

d. it will print 0 1

Question 64) Which of the following represents invalid String initializations in Java? Choose all that apply.

49

a. String s = "1abcde";

b. String s = "ab"c"de";

c. String s = "abc'd'e";

d. String s = "abc\tde";

e. String s = "abc\gde";

Question 65) What will the following program display? Select one correct answer.

```java
public class MyClass {
    public static void main(String args[]) {
        int var = 10;
        System.out.print(++var);
        System.out.println(var++);
    }
}
```

a. 1012

b. 1011

c. 1112

d. 1111

Question 66) What is the output of the following Java code? Choose all that apply.

```java
int intArrayOne[] = {200, 1, 10, 50};
int intArrayTwo[] = new int[2];
intArrayTwo[0] = 300;
```

```
System.arraycopy(intArrayOne, 2, intArrayTwo, 1,
1);
for (int i:intArrayTwo){
    System.out.print(i + " ");
}
```

a) 200 1 10 50 100

b) 200 300

c) 10

d) 10 50

e) 300

f) 300 10

Question 67) What is the output of the following program? Select one answer.

```
class ForTest {
    public static void main(String[] args){
        for(int i=1, j=1; i<3 && j<=3; i++, +
+j){
            System.out.print( i + j);
        }
    }
}
```

a. 23

b. nothing will be displayed

c. 24

d. 235

e. 246

Question 68) Given the following Java program, select the correct statements? Select one correct answer.

```java
public class MyClass {
    public static int count;
    void incCount(int step) {
        this.count += step;                     // 1
    }
    public static void main(String[] args) {
        MyClass c = new MyClass();
        MyClass.count = 0;
        c.count ++;                             // 2
        MyClass.count++;                        // 3
        c.incCount(2);
        System.out.println(MyClass.count);
    }
}
```

a. compilation error at line //1

b. compilation error at line //2

c. compilation error at line //3

d. the program will display 2

e. the program will display 3

f. the program will display 4

Question 69) What is the output of the following program?

52

Select one correct answer.

```
class Base {
    void aMethod() {
        System.out.println("Method in Base class
called");
    }
}
class Derived extends Base {
    void aMethod() {
        System.out.println("Method in Derived
class called");
    }
}
class MyClass {
    public static void main(String[] args)
    {
        Base obj1 = new Derived();
        Derived obj2 = new Derived();
        obj1.aMethod();
        obj2.aMethod();
        obj1 = obj2;
        obj1.aMethod();
    }
}
```

a. compilation error

b. it will display:

```
Method in Derived class called

Method in Derived class called

Method in Derived class called
```

c. it will display:

Method in Base class called

Method in Derived class called

Method in Base class called

d. it will display:

Method in Base class called

Method in Derived class called

Method in Derived class called

Question 70) Given the following Java program, specify which statements below are true. Select one correct answer.

```java
public class MyClass {
    public void MyMethod() {          // 1
        throw new Exception();        // 2
        catch (Exception e) {         // 3
            throw new Exception();
        }
    }
    public static void main(String args[]) {
        new MyClass().MyMethod();     // 4
    }
}
```

a. compilation error at // 1 because MyMethod definition has no "throws" clause

b. compilation error at // 2 because Exception is an abstract class and cannot be instantiated

c. compilation error at // 3 because `catch` must have a corresponding `try` block

d. compilation error at // 4 because `MyMethod` call must be enclosed within a `try-catch` block

Question 71) `MyClass` and `YourClass` are two classes defined in the `package com.oca`. Which of the following are valid constructs inside `YourClass`? Choose all that apply.

a. `import com.oca.MyClass*;`

b. `import com.MyClass;`

c. `import static com.oca.MyClass.*;`

d. `static import com.oca.MyClass.*;`

e. `import java.lang.*;`

f. `import com.oca.MyClass;`

Question 72) What will be the output of the following program? Select one correct answer.

```
public class MyClass {
    public static void main(String args[]) {
        String s = "abc\tde";
        System.out.println(s);
    }
}
```

a. compilation error

b. abcde

c. abc

d. de

e. abc de

f. nothing will be displayed

Question 73) Which of the following are not Java unary operators? Select one correct answer.

a. +

b. -

c. ++

d. &&

e. !

f. ^

Question 74) What is the output of the following program? Select one correct answer.

```
public class MyClass {
    public static void main(String args[]) {
        int arr[] = new int[5];
        for (int i=0; i<5; i++)
            arr[i] = 5-i;
```

```
System.out.println(arr[arr.length]);    // 1
    }
}
```

a. 0

b. 1

c. compilation error at line // 1 as "length" is a method and has to be invoked as arr.length()

d. runtime exception at line // 1

Question 75) Which of the following blocks of code will produce this output? Select one correct answer.

```
1

2 2

3 3 3

4 4 4 4

5 5 5 5 5
```

a.
```
for(int x=1;x<=5;x++){
    for(int y=1;y<x;++y)
        System.out.print(y + " ");
System.out.println("");
}
```

b.
```
for(int x=1;x<=5;x++){
    for(int y=1;y<=x;++y)
        System.out.print(y + " ");
    System.out.println("");
}
```

c.
```
for(int x=1;x<=5;x++){
    for(int y=1;y<=x;++y)
        System.out.print(x + " ");
    System.out.println("");
}
```

d.
```
for(int x=1;x<=5;x++){
    for(int y=1;y<x;++y)
        System.out.print(x + " ");
    System.out.println("");
}
```

Question 76) What is the output of the following code? Select one correct answer.

```
package package1;
public class ClassP1 {}

package package1.package11;
public class ClassP11 {}

package package1.package12;
public class ClassP12 {}

package package2;
import package1.*;
public class ClassP2 {
    public static void main(String[] args){
```

```
        ClassP1 objP1;
        ClassP11 objP11;
        ClassP12 objP12;
    }
}
```

a. no output is produced

b. the code fails to compile

c. the code compiles but an exception is thrown at runtime

d. null is printed three times

Question 77) Which statements are correct regarding the following program? Select one correct answer.

```
public class MyClass {
    static int getFromList(int... values, int
position)
    {
        return values[position];
    }
    public static void main(String[] args)
    {
        int val = getFromList(0,1,2,3,4,2);
        System.out.println(val);
    }
}
```

a. the program will display 2

b. the program will display 1

c. the program will fail to compile as "int... values" is not a valid Java construct

d. the program will fail to compile as "int… values" is not in the last in the list of arguments

Question 78) Given the following code select which of the following of assignments of variables listed below are correct. Choose all that apply.

```
abstract class Base {
    abstract void doMethod1();
    abstract void doMethod2();
    abstract void doMethod3();
}

abstract class Derived1 extends Base {
    void doMethod1() {};
    void doMethod2() {};
}

class Derived2 extends Derived1 {
    void doMethod3() {};
}

class Derived3 extends Derived2 {
}
```

a. Base b = new Base();

b. Base b = new Derived1();

c. Derived1 d1 = new Derived1();

d. Base b = new Derived2();

e. Derived1 d1 = new Derived2();

f. Derived3 d3 = new Derived2();

Question 79) What changes are required in order to make the following Java program to compile? Select one correct answer.

```
public class MyClass {
    public void MyMethod() {                    // 1
        try {
            throw new Exception();
        }
        catch (Exception e) {
            throw new Exception();              // 2
        }
    }
    public static void main(String args[]{ // 3
        new MyClass().MyMethod();               // 4
    }
}
```

a. add a "throws" statement at line // 1

b. add a "throws" statement at line // 1 and another one at line // 3

c. add a "throws" statement at line // 3

d. enclose the call of MyMethod() at line //4 within a try-catch block

Question 80) Which statement is true regarding the following Java program? Select one correct answer.

```
public interface Executable {                   // 1
    void execute();
    void run();
```

61

```
}
class Runner {
      public void run(Executable e) {       // 2
             e.execute();
       }
}
public class MyClass {
      public static void main(String[] args) {
      Runner runner = new Runner();
      Runner.run(() -> System.out.println("Hello
there.")); // 3
      }
}
```

a. implements a correct lambda function in Java at line // 3

b. lambda function at line // 3 must also provide implementation for the "run" method from Executable interface

c. "run" method from class Runner clashes with "run" method from Interface Executable

d. a lambda function cannot be written at line // 3 because interface Executable defines more than one method

Question 81) What is the output of the following Java program? Select one correct answer.

```
class StringTest {
    public static void main(String[] args) {
          String s1 = "abc";
          String s2 = "abc";
          if (s1 == s2) {
                System.out.print("Equal ");
          }
          else
```

```
      {
          System.out.print("Not Equal ");
      }
      if (s1.equals(s2)) {
          System.out.println("Equal");
      }
      else
      {
          System.out.println("Not Equal");
      }
    }
}
```

a. Equal Equal

b. Equal Not Equal

c. Not Equal Equal

d. Not Equal Not Equal

Question 82) Which usage represents a valid way to run the following code? Select one correct answer.

```
public class HelloWorld {
        public static void main(String[] args) {
            System.out.println("Hello world");
        }
}
```

a. javac HelloWorld

b. java HelloWorld

c. javac HelloWorld.java

63

d. java HelloWorld.class

Question 83) What is the output of the following Java program? Select all that apply.

```java
class StringTest {
    public static void main(String[] args) {
        String s1 = "abc";
        String s2 = new String("abc");
        if (s1 == s2) {
            System.out.print("Equal ");
        }
        else
        {
            System.out.print("Not Equal ");
        }
        if (s1.equals(s2)) {
            System.out.println("Equal");
        }
        else
        {
            System.out.println("Not Equal");
        }
    }
}
```

a. Equal Equal

b. Equal Not Equal

c. Not Equal Equal

d. Not Equal Not Equal

Question 84) Which statement is correct regarding the

64

following program? Select one correct answer.

```
public class MyClass {
    static int getFromList(int position , int...
values) // 1
    {
            return values[position];
    }

    public static void main(String[] args)
    {
            int val = getFromList(5, 0, 1, 2, 3,
4);     // 2
            System.out.println(val);
    }
}
```

a. it displays 4

b. compilation error at line // 1

c. compilation error at line // 2

d. it throws `ArrayIndexOutOfBoundsException`

Question 85) What is the output of the following program? Select one correct answer.

```
abstract class Animal {
    public void saySomething() {
        System.out.print(" ");
    }
}
class Cat extends Animal {
    public void saySomething() {
        System.out.print("Meow ");
```

```
        }
    }
class Dog extends Animal {
    public void saySomething() {
        System.out.print("Woof ");
    }
}
class MyClass {
    public static void main(String[] args)
    {
        Animal dog = new Dog();    // 1
        Cat cat = new Cat();       // 2
        dog.saySomething();        // 3
        cat.saySomething();        // 4
        dog = cat;                 // 5
        dog.saySomething();        // 6
    }
}
```

a. compilation error at line // 1

b. compilation error at line // 5

c. `Woof Meow Meow`

d. `Meow Woof`

e. `Meow Meow`

f. `Woof Meow Woof`

Question 86) Examine the following code and select all the incorrect statements.

```
public class HelloWorld {
    public void sayHello() {
```

```
        System.out.println("Hello world");
    }
}
```

a. the code will compile

b. the code will fail to compile as `main` method is not defined

c. the code will fail to execute as `main` method is not defined

d. a default `main` method is provided by the compiler.

e. the code will execute but it will produce no output

Question 87) Which of the following represents correct Java initializations? Choose all that apply.

```
a.  double d = 123.4;
```

```
b.  double d = 123,4;
```

```
c.  double d = 1.234e2;
```

```
d.  double d = 123.4d;
```

```
e.  double d = 123.4f;
```

```
f.  double d = 1234;
```

Question 88) Given the following Java class definitions and object instantiations, which of the following "instanceof" evaluates to true? Choose all that apply.

```
class Parent {}
```

```
class Child extends Parent implements
MyInterface {}
interface MyInterface {}
...
Parent obj1 = new Parent();
Parent obj2 = new Child();
```

a. obj1 instanceof Parent

b. obj1 instanceof Child

c. obj1 instanceof MyInterface

d. obj2 instanceof Parent

e. obj2 instanceof Child

f. obj2 instanceof MyInterface

Question 89) Which of the following statements are true for the following code? Choose all that apply.

```
String myArray[][] = new String[][] {null, {"a",
"b"}, {"0", null}};
```

a. myArray.length is 3

b. myArray[0].length is 0

c. myArray[1].length is 2

d. myArray[2][1] is null

Question 90) Which options are correct equivalents of a following "while" loop? Select all that apply.

```
int x=0;
do{
   System.out.println(x);
   x++;
 }while(x<10);
```

a.

```
int x=0;
while (x<10) {
       System.out.println(x);
       x++;
}
```

b.

```
int x=0;
while (x<=10) {
       System.out.println(x);
       x++;
}
```

c.

```
int x=0;
while (x<10) {
   System.out.println(x++);
}
```

d.

```
int x=0;
for (x=0; x<=10; x++) {
       System.out.println(x);
}
```

Question 91) What statement is true regarding the following class? Select one correct answer.

```
public class MyClass {
    private final int data;
    MyClass(int data) {
        this.data = data;
    }
    public String toString() {
        return "MyClass with data " + data;
    }
}
```

a. this class is a correctly implemented immutable Java class

b. declaring the class as "final public class MyClass", MyClass becomes a correctly implemented mutable class

c. in order for the above to be an immutable class it needs a getter method for the "data" field

d. both b. and c. above are true.

Question 92) What is the correct way of calling the superclass constructor in a class hierarchy? Choose all that apply.

```
class MyBase {
    MyBase() {};
}
```

a.
```
class MyDerived extends MyBase {
    MyDerived() {
        super();
    }
}
```

b.
```
class MyDerived extends MyBase {
```

```
MyDerived() {
    this();
}
}
```

c.
```
class MyDerived extends MyBase {
    MyDerived() {
        MyBase();
    }
}
```

d.
```
class MyDerived extends MyBase {
    MyDerived() {
        MyBase.MyBase();
    }
}
```

e. MyBase **class constructor cannot be called from** MyDerived **class constructor**

f. MyBase **class constructor is invoked automatically when** MyDerived **class constructor is called**

Question 93) Which statement is true regarding the following Java program, assuming the file test.txt doesn't exist in the working folder before running the code? Select one correct answer.

```
import java.io.File;
import java.io.FileReader;
public class MyClass {
  public void MyMethod() {
      try {
          File file = new File("test.txt");
          FileReader fileReader = new
```

71

```
FileReader(file);
    } catch (Exception e) {
    System.out.println("Exception reading
file: " + file.toString());              //1
    } finally {
    System.out.println("Done with file: " +
file.toString());                        //2
    }
}
    public static void main(String args[]) {
        new MyClass().MyMethod();        // 3
        System.out.println("All good");
    }
}
```

a. runtime error at // 1 because the program is attempting to use a file that doesn't exist

b. compilation error at line // 3 because `try-catch` is missing

c. compilation errors at lines // 1 and // 2 because variable `file` is not accessible

d. it will display "All good"

Question 94) Examine the following code and select one correct answer.

```
public class HelloWorld {
    void sayHello();
    public static void main(String[] args) {
        System.out.println("Hello world");
    }
}
```

a. the code will not compile as there is no access modifier

72

specified for the method "sayHello"

b. the code will not compile as the method "sayHello" is not implemented

c. the compiler will provide a default body for the method "sayHello"

d. the code will compile as "sayHello" is not invoked anywhere

Question 95) What will be the output of the following Java program? Select one correct answer.

```
class MyClass {
    public static void main(String[] args){
        int value1 = 2;
        int value2 = 2;
        if(value1 == value2)
            System.out.print("Here1 ");
            if(value1 != value2)
                System.out.print("Here2 ");
                if(value1 >= value2)
                    System.out.print("Here3 ");
                if(value1 < value2)
                    System.out.print("Here4 ");
                    if(value1 <= value2)
                    System.out.print("Here5");
    }
}
```

a. nothing will be displayed

b. Here 1

c. Here1 Here3 Here4

73

d. Here1 Here3 Here5

e. Here1 Here3 Here4 Here5

Question 96) Examine the following class and select all the correct answers.

```
class MyClass {
    private int data;
    private MyClass() {
        data = 0;
    }
    static void doStatic() {
        System.out.println("Static method
invoked!");
    }
}
```

a. compilation error because the only constructor of the class is declared `private`

b. compilation error because because a non static class cannot contain a `static` method

c. class `MyClass` cannot be instantiated

d. the default constructor is used when creating instances of `MyClass`

e.method `doStatic()` can be called using `MyClass.doStatic()`

Question 97) What is the output of the following program? Select one correct answer.

```
class MyClass  {
    @Override                         // 1
    public String toString() {
        super.toString();             // 2
          return "Hi there!";
    }
    public static void main(String[] args) {
        MyClass obj = new MyClass();
        System.out.println(obj.toString());
    }
}
```

a. compilation error at line // 1

b. compilation error at line // 2

c. Hi there!

d. runtime error

Question 98) Examine the following code and select one correct answer.

```
public class NestedVariables {
    int aVar = 3;                       // 1
    public static void main(String[] args) {
        int aVar = 4;                   // 2
        if (aVar == 4)
        {
            int aVar = 5;               // 3
            System.out.println(aVar);
        }
    }
}
```

a. compilation error at line // 1

b. compilation error at line // 2

c. compilation error at line // 3

d. it will print 3

e. it will print 4

f. it will print 5

Question 99) Which of the following represents correct initialization in Java? Select one correct answer:

a. float f = 123.4;

b. float f = 123,4;

c. float f = 1.234e2;

d. float f = 123.4d;

e. float f = 123.4f;

Question 100) What is the output of the following Java program? Select one answer.

```
class MyClass {
    public static void main(String[] args){
        int value1 = 2;
        int value2 = 2;
        if (value1 == value2)
            if (value2 == 3)
                value1++;
        else
            value2++;
```

```
        System.out.print(value1 + " ");
        System.out.println(value2);
    }
}
```

a. 2 2

b. 2 3

c. 3 2

d. 3 3

Question 101) What is the output of the following Java program? Select one answer.

```
public class MyClass {
    public static void main(String[] args) {
        int[][][] arr = { { { 1, 1, 1, 1 }, { 2,
2, 2, 2 } },
            { { 3, 3, 3 }, { 4, 4, 4 }, { 5,
5 } },
            { { 6, 6, 6 }, { 7, 7, 7 }, { 8,
8 }, { 9, 9, 9 } } };

        System.out.println(arr[1][2][1]);
    }
}
```

a. compilation error

b. ArrayIndexOutOfBoundsException

c. 5

d. 3

77

e. 6

Question 102) Which of the following statements are correct regarding the "break" statement? Select all the correct answers:

a. "break" is used to exit the "for", "for-each", "do" and "do-while" loops

b. "break" is used to exit a method

c. "break" is used to exit a {...} delimited Java block of code

d. "break" is used exit a switch statement

e. "break" is used to skip a section of code delimited by the first "continue" statement.

Question 103) What statements are true regarding the following Java class? Select one correct answer.

```
class MyClass {
    private int data;
    public MyClass() {
        data = 0;
    }
    public boolean MyClass(int data) {
        this.data = data;
        return true;
    }
}
```

a. class MyClass can be instantiated as follows: MyClass obj = new MyClass(3);

b. there will be a compilation error when defining "`public void MyClass(int data)`" saying that constructor cannot have a return value;

c. the following line is valid: "`boolean b = new MyClass().MyClass(4);`"

d. the class `MyClass` has two constructors

Question 104) What is the output of the following program? Select one correct answer.

```
class MyClass  {
    int data;
    MyClass(int data) {
        this.data = data;
     }
    public static void main(String[] args) {
        MyClass obj1 = new MyClass(4);
        MyClass obj2 = new MyClass(4);
        if (obj1 == obj2) {
            System.out.println("Objects are
equal ");
        }
        else {
            System.out.println("Objects are not
equal ");
        }
        if (obj1.equals(obj2)) {              // 1
            System.out.println("Objects are
equal ");
        }
        else {
            System.out.println("Objects are not
equal ");
        }
```

```
        }
}
```

a. compilation error at // 1 because "equals" method is not defined

b. "Objects are equal " followed by "Objects are equal"

c. "Objects are not equal " followed by "Objects are equal"

d. "Objects are not equal " followed by "Objects are not equal"

e. can't be determined for certain

Question 105) Which of the following represent correct Java pre defined exception? Choose all that apply.

a. UnsupportedOperationException

b. RuntimeException

c. NullPointerException

d. FloatingPointException

e. InvalidParameterException

f. ArrayIndexOutOfBoundsError

g. MethodNotDefinedException

Question 106) Which statement is true regarding the following

Java program? Select one correct answer.

```
public interface IntfA {
    int FooA(int a);
}
public interface IntfB {
    int FooB(String b);
}
public class MyClass {
    void MyMethod(IntfA i) {};
    void MyMethod(IntfB i) {};

public static void main(String[] args) {
    MyClass class = new MyClass();
    class.MyMethod((a) ->
System.out.println(a)); // 1
    }
}
```

a. it will call "MyMethod(IntfA i)"

b. it will call "MyMethod(IntfB i)"

c. it will call "MyMethod(IntfA i)" followed by "MyMethod(IntfB i)"

d. it will cause compilation error at line // 1

Question 107) Which of the following statements are correct? Choose all that apply.

a. "class" and "object" can be used interchangeably

b. an object is an instance of a class

c. a class is an instance of an object

d. users can define multiple instances of a `class`

e. `objects` have a lifespan but `classes` do not

Question 108) What will the following program display? Select one correct answer.

```
class ConditionalTest {
    static boolean alwaysFalse() {
        System.out.print("3 ");
        return false;
    }
    public static void main(String[] args){
        int data = 1;
        if ((data == 2) && (alwaysFalse() ==
false))
            System.out.print("1 ");
        else
            System.out.print("2 ");
    }
}
```

a. 1

b 2

c. 3 1

d. 2 1

e. 1 3

f. 2 3

Question 109) What statements are true regarding the

following Java class. Select one correct answer.

```
class MyClass {
    private int data = 0;                       // 1
    {
        data = 1;                               // 2
    }
    public  MyClass(int data) {
        this.data = data;
    }
    public int getData() {
        return data;
    }
    public static void main(String[] args)
    {
        MyClass obj = new MyClass(3);
        System.out.println(obj.getData());
    }
}
```

a. compilation error at line //1

b. 3

c. 1

d. compilation error at line // 2

Question 110) Given the following Java classes:

```
class MyBase {
}

class MyDerived1 extends MyBase {
}
```

```
class MyDerived2 extends MyBase {
}
```

And the following class instantiations:

```
MyBase b = new MyBase();

MyDerived1 d1 = new MyDerived1();

MyDerived2 d2 = new MyDerived2();
```

Which of the following statements return true? Choose all that apply.

a. d1 instanceof MyBase

b. d2 instanceof MyBase

c. d1 instanceof MyDerived2

d. b instanceof MyDerived1

e. d1 instanceof b

f. b instanceof d1

g. d2 instanceof d2

Question 111) Which of the following statements are accepted by the Java compiler? Choose all that apply.

a. package com.mockexam.tests;

b. package com.mockexam.*;

c. package tests;

d. package 1;

e. package default;

Question 112) What statements are true regarding the following Java program? Choose all that apply.

```java
public class MyClass {
    public static void main(String[] args) {
        Float f1 = new Float(1);
        if (f1 > 0) {
            Float f2 = new Float(2);
            f2 = 3f;
        }
        System.out.println(f1);   // 1
    }
}
```

a. "f1" and "f2" are eligible for garbage collection when the program starts the execution of line // 1

b. "f2" is already garbaged collected when the program starts the execution of line // 1

c. "f2" is eligible for garbage collection when the program starts the execution of line // 1

d. "f2" is not visible when the program starts the execution of line // 1

Question 113) What is the output of the following Java program? Select one correct answer.

```java
class ConditionalTest {
    static boolean alwaysFalse() {
```

```
        System.out.print("3 ");
        return false;
    }
    public static void main(String[] args){
        int data = 1;
        if ((data == 2) || (alwaysFalse() ==
false))
            System.out.print("1 ");
        else
            System.out.print("2 ");
    }
}
```

a. 1

b. 2

c. 3 1

d. 2 1

e. 1 3

f. 2 3

Question 114) What is the output of the following Java program? Select one correct answer.

```
import java.util.ArrayList;
public class MyClass {
    public static void main(String[] args) {
        ArrayList<Integer> list = new
ArrayList<Integer>();
        list.add(0);
        list.add(1);
        list.add(1,2);
```

```
        list.add(3);
        System.out.println(list);
    }
}
```

a. [0, 1, 2, 3]

b. [0, 2, 1, 3]

c. [3, 2, 1, 0]

d. [3, 1, 2, 0]

Question 115) What is the final value of "val" at the end of the "for" loop? Select one correct answer.

```
int val = 1;
for (int i = 0; i<10; i++) {
    if (i % 3 == 0)
        continue;
    val += i;
}
```

a. 1

b. 37

c. 28

d. 27

e. 46

Question 116) Which statements are true regarding the

following Java class? Select one correct answer.

```java
class MyClass {
    private static int data = 0;
    public static void incrementData() {
        data++;
    }
    public void decrementData() {
        data--;                              // 1
    }
    public static void main(String[] args)
    {
            MyClass obj = new MyClass();
            obj.incrementData();             // 2
            MyClass.incrementData();
            MyClass.decrementData();         // 3
            System.out.println(data);

    }
}
```

a. compilation error at line // 1 as "data" is accessed without class name (MyClass.data)

b. compilation error at line // 2 as static method incrementData() is invoked using an object

c. compilation error at line // 3 as non static method is invoked using class name

d. 0

e. 1

Question 117) Given the following Java class hierarchy:

```java
class Base {
```

```
}

class Derived1 extends Base {
}

class Derived2 extends Base {
}
```

And the following class instantiations:

```
Base b = new Base();

Derived1 d1 = new Derived1();

Derived2 d2 = new Derived2();
```

Which of the following Java statements are correct? Select one correct answer.

a. `b = d1;`

b. `d2 = b;`

c. `d1 = (Base)b;`

d. `d2 = d1;`

e. `d1 = (Derived1)d2;`

Question 118) Which of the following statements regarding Java exceptions are true? Select all that apply.

a. "`finally`" block always executes

b. the order of the exceptions caught in the catch blocks is never important

c. a checked exception is a subclass of `java.lang.RuntimeException`

d. `java.lang.Throwable` is the base class of all exceptions

e. an exception can be re - thrown in the `catch` block

f. exceptions are divided into three categories: checked exceptions, runtime (or unchecked exceptions) and errors

Question 119) Which of the following statements is correct? Select one correct answer.

```
package
this_is_a_very_long_package_name_for_1st_oracle_
exam;
```

a. package declaration is incorrect because it starts with a reserved keyword ("this")

b. package declaration is incorrect because it contains an invalid character ("_")

c. package definition is incorrect because it contains a digit ("1")

d. package definition is correct

e. Java compiler restricts the length of package names to 25 characters

f. Java compiler expects a package name in format: "com.domain.package_name"

Question 120) Given the following class and interface definitions, select all the expressions that evaluate to true.

```
class Parent {}

class Child extends Parent implements
MyInterface {}

interface MyInterface {}

class Cousin implements MyInterface{}

...

Parent parent = new Parent();

Child child = new Child();

Cousin cousin = new Cousin();
```

a. parent instanceof Object

b. MyInterface instanceof Object

c. Child instanceof Child

d. Child instanceof Parent

e. cousin instanceof Parent

f. child instanceof Parent

91

Question 121) Which statements are true regarding the following Java class? Select one correct answer.

```java
class MyClass {
    private static int data = 0;
    public static void incrementData() {
        data++;
    }
    public void decrementData() {
        data--;                                // 1
    }
    public static void main(String[] args)
    {
            MyClass obj = new MyClass();
            obj.incrementData();         // 2
            MyClass.incrementData();
            obj.decrementData();
            System.out.println(data);
    }
}
```

a. compilation error at line // 1 as static member "data" is accessed without class name (MyClass.data)

b. compilation error at line // 2 as static method incrementData() is invoked using a reference variable

c. 0

d. 1

Question 122) Examine the following Java program and select one correct answer.

```java
public class NestedComments {
    public static void main(String[] args) {
```

```
/*
//                    int aVar = 5;      // comment
 */
             System.out.println("Hello world!");


     }
}
```

a. the program will compile with no errors

b. the program will not compile as the compiler does not allow mixing end-of-line comments ("//") with multiline comments ("/* ... */")

c. the program will not compile as 2 end-of-line comments ("//") are present on the same line

d. the program will compile but it will also generate a warning about the use of nested comments in the code.

Question 123) Which objects are eligible for garbage collection when the code reaches line // 9 in the program below? Select one correct answer.

```
public class MyClass {
    public static void main(String[] args) {
         Float f1 = new Float(1);        // 1
         Float f2 = new Float(2);        // 2
         Float f3 = new Float(3);        // 3
         f1 = f2;                        // 4
         Float f11 = f1;                 // 5
         f1 = null;                      // 6
         f2 = null;                      // 7
         f3 = null;                      // 8
         System.out.println("Who's up for garbage
collection?");// 9
```

```
        }
}
```

a. object created at line //1

b. object created at line // 2

c. object created at line // 3

d. objects created at line // 1 and line // 2

e. objects created at line // 1 and line // 3

f. objects created at line // 2 and line // 3

g. none

Question 124) What will the following program display? Select one correct answer.

```
class BitTest {
    public static void main(String[] args) {
        int bitmask = 0x000F;
        int val = 0x2222;
        System.out.println(val & bitmask << 4);
    }
}
```

a. nothing. Compilation error

b. nothing. Runtime error

c. 32

d. 16

e. 0x20

Question 125) What is the output of the following program? Select one correct answer.

```
public class MyClass {
    public static void main(String[] args) {
        Integer arr[] = new Integer[5];
        System.out.println(arr[0]);
    }
}
```

a. 0

b. null

c. unspecified

d. compilation error

e. runtime error

Question 126) What is the output of the following program? Select one correct answer.

```
class MyClass {
        public static void main(String[] args){
            int count = 1;
            for (int i = 0; i<10; i++) {
again:
            for (int j = 0; j<10; j++)
            if (i == j)
                break again;
            count++;
            }
```

```
        System.out.println(count);
    }
}
```

a. compilation error

b. 10

c. 11

d. 46

e. 45

Question 127) Which of the following are not Java keywords? Choose all that apply.

a. volatile

b. transient

c. goto

d. friend

e. import

f include

g. expand

h. this

i native

Question 128) Which statements are true regarding the following Java class? Select one correct answer.

```
class MyClass {
    private static int data = 0;


    private void incrementData() {
        data++;                             // 1
    }
    private void decrementData() {
        data--;                             // 2
    }
    public static void doOperation(boolean
increment) {
        if (increment == true)
            incrementData();                // 3
        else
            decrementData();                // 4
    }
    public static void main(String[] args)
    {
        MyClass obj = new MyClass();
        obj.doOperation(true);              // 5
    }
}
```

a. compilation errors at //1 and //2 as non-static methods cannot access static members of a class

b. compilation errors at //3 and //4 as static methods cannot access non-static members of a class

c. compilation error at //5 a static method cannot be accessed using a reference variable

d. none of the above

Question 129) What will be the output of the following program? Select one correct answer.

```
class Base {
}
class Derived1 extends Base {
    void Method() {
    System.out.println("Method1");
    }
}
class Derived2 extends Base {
    void Method() {
        System.out.println("Method2");
    }
    public static void main(String[] args) {
        Derived1 d1 = new Derived1();
        Derived2 d2 = new Derived2();
        d1 = (Derived1)d2;                 // 1
        d1.Method();
    }
}
```

a. compilation error at line // 1

b. it will throw `java.lang.ClassCastException`

c. it will display "Method1"

d. it will display "Method2"

Question 130) Which of the following implement checked exceptions? Choose all that apply.

a. class A extends RuntimeException

b. class A extends Throwable

c. class A extends Exception

d. class A extends IOException

Question 131) What is the output of the following code? Select one correct option:

```
public class MyClass {
    public static void main(String args[]) {
        int i = 10;
        {
            i++;
            System.out.println(i);
        }
        {

            i= i-1;
            System.out.println(i);
        }
    }
}
```

a. compilation error due to erroneous use of the brackets "{", "}" in the code

b. 10 10

c. 11 10

d. 10 9

e. 11 9

Question 132) What is the output of the following program? Select one correct answer.

```
public class MyClass {
    public static void main(String[] args) {
        String s = "hello";
        s = new
StringBuilder(s).append(s).reverse().substring(0
, 4);
        System.out.println(s);
    }
}
```

a. hello

b. olle

c. olleh

d. olleho

e. compilation error

Question 133) What types can be used in the "switch" statement's expression? Choose all that apply.

a. byte, float, char

b. int, enum, short

c. String, char, byte

d. double, char, int

e. boolean, int, byte

Question 134) What is the output of the following Java program? Select one correct answer.

```java
import java.util.ArrayList;
import java.util.List;

public class MyClass {
    public static void main(String[] args) {
        List list = new ArrayList();      // 1
        list.add(0);
        list.add("one");                  // 2
        list.add(1, new Float(0.1));
        list.add(5);
        list.remove(3);                   // 3
        System.out.println(list);
    }
}
```

a. error at // 1 because element type is not specified

b. error at // 2 because we attempt to add a String in the same array list that already contains an integer

c. error at // 3 because "remove" is not a method of List Interface

d. it will print [0, 0.1, one]

e. it will print [0, 0.1, one, 5]

Question 135) Which of the following statements are true regarding "break" and "goto" statements in Java? Choose all that apply.

a. there is no difference between these two statements

b. there is no difference, but only when used inside loops

c. "break" can have both labeled and non labeled versions whereas "goto" can only have labeled version

d. "break" used outside a loop causes compilation error

e. "goto" is a reserved Java keyword but not currently used

Question 136) What class cannot be instantiated? Select all that apply.

a. an abstract class

b. a class with at least one abstract method

c. a class with static methods only

d. a class that implements an interface

Question 137) What is the output of the following program? Select one correct answer.

```
class Base {
    Base() {
        System.out.println("Constructor Base");
    }
    void Method() {
        System.out.println("Method Base");
    }
}
class Derived extends Base {
```

```
    Derived() {
        System.out.println("Constructor
Derived");
    }
    void Method() {
        System.out.println("Method Derived");
    }
}
class MyClass {
    public static void main(String[] args) {
        Derived d = new Derived();
        d.Method();
    }
}
```

a.
```
Constructor Derived
Method Derived
```

b.
```
Constructor Base
Constructor Derived
Method Derived
```

c.
```
Constructor Base
Constructor Derived
MethodBase
Method Derived
```

d.
```
Constructor Derived
Constructor Base
MethodBase
Method Derived
```

Question 138) Given the following statements, select the correct options.

a. a `try` block can define multiple `finally` blocks

b. a `try` block can be followed by multiple `catch` blocks

c. both Error and checked exceptions need to be part of a method signature

d. `NullPointerException` is a thrown by the JVM when trying to access a method or a variable with a null value

Question 139) What is the output of the following program?

```
public class MyClass {
    public static void main(String args[]) {
        int i = 1, j = 2;
        int r = i++ + 1 + 2*j;
        System.out.println(r);
    }
}
```

a. compilation error

b. 0

c. 3

d. 4

e. 5

f. 6

Question 140) What is the output of the following code? Select one correct answer:

```
String month = "Dec";
switch(month) {
   case "Dec":
   case "Jan":
   case "Feb": System.out.println("Winter
months");
   case null: System.out.println("Other...");
}
```

a. it will print nothing

b. it will print Winter months

c. it will print Other

d. the code won't compile

Questions and Answers

Q&A 1) Which of the following are correct? Choose all that apply.

a.
```
import java.lang.*;
class Test {
}
```

b.
```
import java.lang.*;
package com.ocjpa.mockexams;
class Test {
}
```

c.
```
package com.ocjpa.mockexams;
package com.ocjpa.learning;
import java.util.*;
public class Test {
}
```

d.
```
package com.ocjpa.mockexams;
import java.util.ArrayList;
import java.util.*;
public class Test {
}
```

e.
```
package com.ocjpa.mockexams.*;
public class Test {
}
```

106

Correct answer: a, d.

b. is incorrect because a package statement (if present) must be the first statement in the file.

c. is incorrect because a class definition cannot contain multiple package statements.

e. is incorrect because `package com.ocjpa.mockexams.*` is syntactically incorrect.

Q&A 2) What is the result of evaluating 2^2 expression? Select one correct answer.

a. 0

b. 2

c. 4

d. None of the above

Correct answer: a.

In Java the "^" operator represents the bitwise exclusive OR operator. The results of 2^2 is equal to 0 according to the truth table for this operator:

0 ^ 0 = 0

1 ^ 0 = 1

0 ^ 1 = 1

1 ^ 1 = 0

The binary representation of "2" is "10". Therefore "2 ^ 2" becomes "10 ^ 10" which is 0 according to the above table.

Q&A 3) Which of the following represent correct method declarations? Choose all that apply.

a. `int foo(int a,b)`

b. `int foo(int a, int b)`

c. `int foo(int a=0, int b)`

d. `int foo(int a, int b=0)`

e. `int foo(int a=0, int b=0)`

f. `int foo(int… a)`

Correct answer: b, f.

c.,d.,e. are incorrect as Java methods cannot have default values.

a. is incorrect because is not syntactically correct. Java does not allow specifying a list of parameters names for one type.

Q&A 4) Given the following Java classes select the correct statements. Choose all that apply.

```
package com.ocjpa.mockexams;
```

```
class Base {
    private int private_data;
    protected int protected_data;
    public int public_data;
    int data;
    private void doPrivateMethod() {}
    protected void doProtectedMethod() {}
    public void doPublicMethod() {}
    final void doFinalMethod() {}
}
class Foo extends Base {
}
```

a. "private_data" is visible in class Foo

b. "protected_data" is visible in in class Foo

c. "public_data" is visible in class Foo

d. "data" is visible in class Foo

e. "doPrivateMethod()" is visible in class Foo

f. "doProtectedMethod()" is visible in class Foo

g. "doPublicMethod()" is visible in class Foo

h. "doFinalMethod()" is visible in class Foo

Correct answer: b,c, d, f, g, h.

Public and protected members are visible in derived classes from the same or separate packages.

The members with no access modifier have "package accessibility" meaning that these are accessible to classes and interfaces defined in the same package.

Q&A 5) Which of the following constructs are incorrect? Select one answer.

a.
```
public class Circle {
    public double getCircleArea(double radius) {
        return Math.PI*radius*radius;
    }
}
```

b.
```
import static java.lang.Math.PI;
public class Circle {
    public double getCircleArea(double radius) {
        return PI*radius*radius;
    }
}
```

c.
```
import static java.lang.Math.*;
public class Circle {
    public double getCircleArea(double radius) {
        return PI*radius*radius;
    }
}
```

d.
```
import java.lang.Math.*;
public class Circle {
    public double getCircleArea(double radius) {
        return PI*radius*radius;
    }
}
```

Correct answer: d.

To import all static members of a class an import static statement must be used.

Q&A 6) What is the number of bytes used to represent a Java primitive type int? Select one correct answer.

a. it is dependent on the Java compiler

b. it is dependent on the operating system

c. 2

d. 4

e. 8

f. none of the above

Correct answer: d.

See the table below for the number of bytes used in representing Java data type primitives:

Data Type	Size (bits)	Size (bytes)
byte	8 bits	1
short	16 bits	2

| int | 32 bits | 4 |
| long | 64 bits | 8 |

Q&A 7) What is the output of the following Java program? Select one answer.

```
public class MyClass {
    public static void main(String[] args) {
        int sel = 0;
        switch(sel) {
            case 0: System.out.print(0);
            case 1: System.out.print(1); break;
            case 2: System.out.print(2);
            case 3: System.out.print(3); break;
            default: System.out.print(4);
        }
    }
}
```

a. 0

b. 01

c .012

d. 0123

e. 01234

f. none of the above

Correct answer: b.

For a switch statement, the control enters the case labels when the first match is found.

The control then falls through the remaining case labels until it reaches the end of the construct or until a "break" is found.

In our example, the first matching label is "case 0", therefore "0" will be displayed first. It will then execute the code for next case label: "1" is displayed and then the execution is terminated as a break statement is encountered.

Q&A 8) Given the following Java program select the correct answer.

```
class MyClass {
        void swap(int a, int b) {
            int tmp;
            tmp = a;
            a = b;
            b = tmp;
        }
        public static void main(String[] args){
            int a=1, b=2, c=3;
            swap(a,b);
            swap(b,c);
            System.out.println(a + " " + b + " " +
c);
        }
}
```

a. it will produce a compilation error

b. it will display: 1 2 3

c. it will display: 2 3 1

d. it will display: 2 1 3

Correct answer: a.

The program is trying to invoke a non static method (swap) from a static method (main). This is not possible and the Java compiler will flag this as an error.

Q&A 9) What is the output of the following Java program? Select one correct answer.

```
class Base {
    int data = 1;
    int getData() {
        return data;
    }
}
class Derived extends Base {
    int data = 2;
}
class MyClass {
    public static void main(String[] args)
    {
            Base base = new Base();
            Derived derived = new Derived();
            System.out.print(base.getData());
            System.out.println(derived.getData());
    }
}
```

a. 11

b. 12

c. 22

d. compilation error because "data" from class Base is duplicated in class Derived.

Correct answer: a.

For both objects, **base** and **derived**, the getData() method refers to the "data" field defined in the Base class which is initialized to 1.

In this example one can say "data" in class Derived hides "data" defined in class Base.

Q&A 10) Which of the following statements is true? Select one correct answer.

a. all the errors and exceptions extend the class java.lang.Throwable

b. Java programs must handle all the exceptions

c. "Error" and "RuntimeException" means the same thing and can be used interchangeably

d. user defined exceptions can only be checked exceptions

Correct answer: b.

a – true. Both java.lang.Error and java.lang.Exception inherit from java.lang.Throwable

b – false. Only checked exceptions must be explicitly dealt with in the code. The program may choose not to handle unchecked exceptions. An error can be caught by an exception handler but it is not recommended.

c – false. "Error" and "RuntimeException" describe different types of Java exceptions. The first category describes JVM internal errors (e.g "out for memory" or "stack overflow") whereas the runtime exceptions are usually the result of an inappropriate handling by the code (e.g "division by zero")

d – false. A Java programmer can choose whether a user defined exception is a checked or an unchecked exception by either extending the "RuntimeException" or the "Exception" class.

Q&A 11) What is the output of the following Java program? Select one correct answer.

```
import static java.lang.Math.*;
public class Circle {
    public double getCircleArea(double radius) {
        return PI*radius*radius;
    }
    public static void main(String[] args){
        System.out.println(getCircleArea(10));
    }
}
```

a. the program will fail to compile

b. it will print 314.1592653589793

c. it will compile correctly but will give an error at runtime

d. it will print 3.141592653589793

Correct answer: a.

The code will fail to compile because a static method cannot access any of the non-static members of a class.

Q&A 12) What is the output of the following Java program? Select one correct answer.

```java
public class MyClass {
    public static void main(String[] args) {
        int sel = 0;
        switch(sel) {
            case 0: System.out.print(0);
            case 1: System.out.print(1);
            case 2: System.out.print(2);
            case 3: System.out.print(3);
            default: System.out.print(4);
        }
    }
}
```

a. 0

b. 0123

c. 01234

d. none of the above

Correct answer: c.

The control enters the first case label, **case** 0, then it falls through the remaining case labels until it reaches the end of the construct, as no **break** statement is found.

Therefore the program will print: 01234

Q&A 13) What happens when the following Java code is compiled and run? Select one correct answer.

```
package com.ocjpa.mockexams;
public class TestMultipleMain {
    public static void main(String args) {
        System.out.println("First main method");
    }
    public static void main(String[] args) {
        System.out.println("Second main
method");
    }
}
```

a. the program will fail to compile

b. the program will print "First main method" followed by "Second main method"

c. the program will print "First main method"

d. the program will print "Second main method"

e. the program will produce an error at runtime

f. none of the above

Correct answer: d.

The class contains two overloaded methods for main. However only the second method has the correct signature of the main method that is recognized by JVM as the starting point for the program execution.

Q&A 14) What is the range of values that can be specified for Java primitive type `int`? Select one correct answer.

a. this is compiler dependent

b. this is operating system dependent

c. -2^{31} to $2^{31} - 1$

d. any integer value can be used

Correct answer: c.

Java type `int` is represented using 32 bits (4 bytes) and its range of values from -2^{31} to $2^{31} - 1$.

Q&A 15) What is the output the following program? Select one correct answer.

```
public class MyClass {
    public static void main(String[] args) {
        int sel = 0;
        switch(sel) {
            case "0": System.out.print(0);
            case "1": System.out.print(1);
            break;
```

119

```
case "2": System.out.print(2);
case "3": System.out.print(3);
break;
default: System.out.print(4);
}
        }
    }
}
```

a. 0

b. 01

c. 4

d. the program will display nothing

e. compilation error

Correct answer: e.

The variable `sel` is declared is as `int` and all the labels from `case` statement contain `String` expressions. The Java compiler will flag this as an error as one cannot compare an `int` variable with a `String`.

Q&A 16) Given the following statements select all the correct answers?

a. for a "`while`" loop the exit condition is evaluated before entering the loop

b. the code inside the "`do - while`" loop is executed at least once

c. the code inside the "while" loop is executed at least once

d. "do - while" and "while" can only define a single line of code to execute

Correct answer: a, b.

The "while" loop evaluates the condition before the execution of the code in its body, whereas the "do-while" loop evaluates the condition after the execution of the code in its body. Therefore the code inside the "do-while" loop is executed at least once.

c) is not correct. If the first evaluation of the exit condition returns false, the code in the loop body is never executed.

d) is also false, as both loops can define a code block to execute using curly braces {}.

Q&A 17) What is the output when the following code is compiled and run? Select one correct answer.

```
class classA{
    private int memberClassA;
    public void setNumber(int number){
        memberClassA = number;
    }
}
public class Test{
    public static void main(String[] args) {
        classA  objA = new classA();
        objA.memberClassA = 10;
        System.out.println(objA.memberClassA);
        objA.setNumber(20);
        System.out.println(objA.memberClassA);
```

```
        }
}
```

a. It will fail to compile

b. It will compile but fail to execute

c. It will print 10 twice

d. It will print 10 followed by 20

Correct answer: a.

Private members of a class are not accessible from outside. As "memberClassA" is a private member of "classA", it is not accessible from any another class. Hence it also not accessible from "Test" class.

Q&A 18) Given the following Java program, select the correct answer.

```
class MyClass {
        static void swap(int var1, int var2) {
            int tmp;
            tmp = var1;
            var1 = var2;
            var2 = tmp;
        }
        public static void main(String[] args){
            int a=1, b=2, c=3;
            swap(a,b);
            swap(b,c);
            System.out.println(a + " " + b + " " +
c);
```

```
        }
}
```

a. it will produce a compilation error

b. it will display: 1 2 3

c. it will display: 2 3 1

d. it will display: 2 1 3

Correct answer: b.

In Java primitive variables are passed by value. Thus the `swap` method will receive a copy of the original value and not a reference to the original value itself. As a result, the variables **a**, **b** and **c** from the main method will not change and the program will display: 1 2 3.

Q&A 19) Assuming the classes below are in the same package, which of the following statements is correct? Select one correct answer.

```
class Base {
    private int data;
    void setData(int data) {
        this.data = data;
    }
    int getData() {
        return this.data;
    }
}
class Derived extends Base {
    void setData(int data) {                   // 1
```

123

```
        super.setData(data);                    // 2
    }
    int getData() {                             // 3
        return super.getData();                 // 4
    }
}
```

a. error at //1 and //2 because the methods in derived class have the same name as in the base class

b. error at //2 because the "data" passed as parameter clashes with the object field "data"

c. error at //2 and //4 because the syntax used to call a base class method is incorrect

d. error at //2 and //4 because "setData" and "getData" are not marked as "public" and they are not accessible in class Derived

e. error at //2 and //4 because the Derived class is ultimately trying to access the private object field "data" of the Base class

f. none of the above

Correct answer: f.

a. False. This is the correct way to override methods in Java.

b. False. "data" here is the method parameter and not the object field.

c. False. This is how we refer to overridden base class methods from a derived class.

124

d. False. If no access modifier is specified for a member of a class, that member has package accessibility. This means the member is accessible to all classes defined in the same package.

e. False. The class Derived only interacts with the public methods getData and setData of the Base class which is perfectly fine.

Q&A 20) What is the output of the following Java program? Select one correct answer.

```
public class MyClass {
      int data = 0;
      public void Method3() throws Exception {
            throw new Exception();
      }
      public void Method2() throws Exception {
            Method3();
            data++;
      }
      public void Method1() {
            try {
                  data++;
                  Method2();
                  data++;
            }
            catch (Exception e) {
                  data++;
            }
            finally {
                  data++;
            }
         System.out.println(data);
      }
      public static void main(String args[]) {
         new MyClass().Method1();
      }
```

125

}

a. 0

b. 1

c. 2

d. 3

e. 4

f. 5

Correct answer: d.

data is initialized with 0 then it is incremented in the following places:

```
public class MyClass {
        int data = 0;
        public void Method3() throws Exception {
                throw new Exception();
        }
        public void Method2() throws Exception {
                Method3();
                data++;     // this line will not
execute as Method3() throws an exception and the
control is transferred to the catch block of
Method1()
        }
        public void Method1() {
                try {
                        data++;     // data is
incremented for first time
```

```
            Method2();
            data++;      // data not
incremented, code not executed
            }
            catch (Exception e) {
                data++;      // data is
incremented for the second time
            }
            finally {
                data++;      // data is
incremented for the third as the finally block
is always executed
            }
        System.out.println(data);
        }
        public static void main(String args[]) {
            new MyClass().Method1();
        }
}
```

Note that when an exception is thrown the next statements are no longer executed and the control is transferred to the first matching "catch" followed by the "finally" if present.

Q&A 21) What is the output of the following code? Select one correct answer.

```
class classA{
    int memberClassA = 20;
    public void setNumber(int memberClassA){
        memberClassA = memberClassA;
    }
    public int getNumber(){
        return memberClassA;
    }
}
public class TestMultipleMain {
```

```
    public static void main(String[] args) {
        classA  objA = new classA();
        objA.setNumber(30);
        System.out.println(objA.getNumber());
    }
}
```

a. the program will not compile

b. runtime exception

c. it will print 20

d. it will print 30

e. no output is produced

Correct answer: c.

As the method "setNumber" uses a parameter with the same name as the name of an instance member, hence the assignment statement "memberClassA = memberClassA;" refers to the argument memberClassA and not the instance member memberClassA. Therefore calling the method setNumber has no effect on the instance field memberClassA which remains with value of 20.

Q&A 22) What will the following program print when trying to compiled and execute it? Select one correct answer.

```
public class MyClass {
    public static void main(String args[]) {
        int i = 1;
```

```
     System.out.println(++i+i++);
     }
}
```

a. compilation error

b. 1

c. 3

d. 4

e. 5

Correct answer: d.

The general rule is the following:

- when ++ is used in prefix notation, the value is incremented before is used in the expression

- when ++ is used in postfix notation, its value is incremented after it has been used in the expression

In our example, i is incremented from 1 to 2 due to the "++i" construction, then the new value, 2, is used for the addition.

The program will therefore print 4, although the value of i at the end of the program will be 3.

Q&A 23) Given the following statements select all the correct answers.

129

a. when a new object is created using the new keyword, memory is allocated for the new instance of the class

b. the default constructor is always called prior to returning the reference to the new object

c. a constructor is called to perform the initialization of the object

d. a reference to the object is returned

Correct answer: a, c, d.

a. is correct as always new memory will be allocated in order to "host" the new object.

b. is incorrect as the default constructor will only be called when no other constructor is provided.

c. is correct as always a matching constructor will be called to perform the initialization of the object.

d. is also correct as the ultimate purpose of the new operator is to return a reference to the newly created object.

Q&A 24) Which of the following are correct declarations of a top level Java class? Select all that apply.

a. public class MyClass{}

b. public static class MyClass{}

c. private class MyClass{}

d. class MyClass{}

e. protected class MyClass{}

Correct answer: a, d.

A top level class is a class that is not defined within another class.

static, private and protected modifiers cannot be used for top level classes.

Q&A 25) Why does the following class break the principles of data encapsulation? Select one correct answer.

```
public class Circle {
    public float radius = 5;
    static final double PI = 3.14;
    void setRadius(double radius) {
        this.radius = radius;
    }
    double getRadius() {
        return this.radius;
    }
}
```

a. there are no get/set methods for PI

b. "radius" is declared as "public"

c. PI has the "static" modifier

d. PI is "final" so it cannot longer be modified

e. the class has no constructor

f. radius is not initialized in any constructor

Correct answer: b.

A well encapsulated class does not expose its internal components to the outside world, but it provides a set of methods to access these elements.

By declaring radius as public, this field becomes directly exposed to the users of the class bypassing any getter and setter methods provided.

Q&A 26) Given the following statements, select one correct answer.

```
class Base {
    void doMethodA() {
        System.out.println("Method A in Base");
    }
    void doMethodB() {                      // 1
        System.out.println("Method B in Base");
    }
}
class Derived extends Base {
    void doMethodA() {
        System.out.println("Method A in
Derived");
    }
    int doMethodB() {                       // 2
        System.out.println("Method B in
Derived");
        return 0;
```

```
        }
    }
class MyClass {
    public static void main(String[] args)
    {
        Derived d = new Derived();
        d.doMethodA();
        d.doMethodB();
    }
}
```

a. the program will print "Method A in Base" followed by "Method B in Base"

b. the program will print "Method A in Base" followed by "Method B in Base"

c. the program will print "Method A in Base" followed by "Method B in Derived"

d. compilation error at line // 2

Correct answer: d.

"doMethodB()" methods have the same signature in both Base and Derived classes. Therefore, the compiler will understand this as an attempt of method overriding. However the return types are different causing the compilation to fail.

Q&A 27) Given the following Java program:

```
public class CmdLineParams {
```

```
    public static void main(String[] args) {
        System.out.print(args.length+" ");//
Line 1
        System.out.print(args[0]+" ");// Line 2
        System.out.print(args[1]+" ");// Line 3
    }
}
```

What is the output if the program is run with the following command:

java CmdLineParams 12 3

Select one correct answer.

a. 3 12 3

b. 3 CmdLineParams 12

c. 3 1 2

d. 2 12 3

e. 2 CmdLineParams 12 3

Correct answer: d.

Line 1 prints the length of the array passed in the command line (args). The array has 2 elements, 12 and 3, therefore its length is 2.

Line 2 prints the first element passed as parameter (the first element of the array args), which is 12. Line 3 prints the second element passed as parameter (the second element of the array args), which is 3.

Q&A 28) Which of the following statements are true? Choose all that apply.

a. "static variables" are also known as "class variables"

b. "instance variables" are also known as "static fields"

c. static members can access non static methods and variables

d. static members can be accessed even if no instances of the class are created

Correct answer: a, d.

a - static members are also known as class members.

b - instance variables belong to individual objects and are different from static variables or fields which belong to the class.

c - static members cannot access non static members of a class.

d - this is true, static members belong to the class and therefore can be accessed even if no object has been created.

Q&A 29) Which of the following are correct array declarations in Java? Select all that apply.

```
a. int a[5][];
```

```
b. int a[][];
```

c. `int[5][] a;`

d. `int[5][5] a;`

e. `int a[5][5];`

f. `int[][] a;`

g. `int[]a[];`

Correct answer: b, f, g.

All the other answers are false because the array size cannot be specified when doing the array declaration.

Q&A 30) Given the following Java program, select all the correct answers.

```java
class DoWhileDemo {
    public static void main(String[] args){
        int count = 0;
        do {
            System.out.print(count);
            count++;
            while(count > 0) {
                --count;
                System.out.print(count);
            }
        } while (count < 11);
        System.out.println(count);
    }
}
```

a. the program will print 10 an infinite number of times

b. the program will print 0 an infinite number of times

c. at the end of the program the value of count is 12

d. at the end of the program the value of count is 11

Correct answer: b.

The program will enter the inner loop with `count` = 1. The body of the inner loop will be executed once and it will display "0". These steps are repeated an infinite number of times as the value of count will never exceed the value of 1.

Q&A 31) Given the following class, select the all the correct answers.

```
class MyJavaClass {
    private String field1;
    private String field2;
    private int numericField;
    MyJavaClass(String field1) {              // 1
        this.field1 = field1;
    }
    MyJavaClass(String field2) {              // 2
        this.field2 = field2;
    }
    MyJavaClass(String f1,   String f2) {    // 3
        this.field1 = f1;
        this.field2 = f2;
    }
    MyJavaClass(String f1,   String f2, int num)
{   // 4
        this.numericField = num;
        this(f1, f2);                         // 5
```

```
    }
    MyJavaClass(String f1,    int num, String f2) {
// 6
         this.numericField = num;
         this.field1 = f1;
         this.field2 = f2;
    }
}
```

a. constructors cannot be overloaded in Java

b. overloaded constructors at line //1 and line //2 are not correct as "field1" and "field2" passed as parameters have the same name as the class fields

c. overloaded constructors at line //1 and line //2 are not correct as they have the same signature

d. a constructor cannot be invoked using the statement in line //5

e. the constructors defined at lines //4 and //6 are identical

Correct answer: c, d.

c. The names of the method parameters are ignored when the signature is generated. The following elements are used to generate the signature of a constructor or method:

- method/constructor name

- number of parameters

- parameters type

- order of parameters

Therefore, the constructors at lines //1 and //2 have the same signature

d. is correct because the call to another constructor must be the first statement. The code below shows a correct implementation of the constructor defined at line // 4.

```
MyJavaClass(String f1,   String f2, int num)
{   // 4
        this(f1, f2);
        this.numericField = num;
}
```

Q&A 32) Which of the following statements are true regarding the @Override annotation? Select one correct answer.

a. it is just some note in the code reading a method that we want to override and it has no effect on compilation

b. it controls whether or not a particular method is overloaded

c. it forces the compiler to check that method overrides a method from the base class

d. it allows to override a method from the base class but using a different name

Correct answer: c.

The @Override annotation is used to make sure that a method with similar signature exists in the base class. Using this annotation is seen a good coding practice when we intend to override a method. It also increases the code readability.

Q&A 33) What is the output of the following Java program assuming that the file "test.txt" does not exist? Select one correct answer.

```java
import java.io.File;
import java.io.FileNotFoundException;
import java.io.FileReader;
import java.io.IOException;
class MyFileException extends
FileNotFoundException {}
public class MyClass {
    public void Method() {
        try {
            File file = new File("test.txt");
            FileReader fileReader = new
FileReader(file); // 1
        }
        catch (MyFileException e) {
            System.out.println("I was here 1");
        }
        catch (IOException e) {
            System.out.println("I was here 2");
        }
        catch (Exception e) {
            System.out.println("I was here 3");
        }
        finally {
            System.out.println("I was here 4");
        }
    }
    public static void main(String args[]) {
        new MyClass().Method();
    }
}
```

a. `"I was here 1"`

b. "I was here 2"

c. "I was here 3"

d. `"I was here 4"`

e. "I was here 1" followed by "I was here 4"

f. "I was here 2" followed by "I was here 4"

g. "I was here 3" followed by "I was here 4"

Correct answer: f.

The program will throw "FileNotFoundException" at line // 1.

An exception is caught in a certain catch block if:

1)   The catch parameter exactly matches the exception type

2)   The type of the catch parameter is a base of the exception type

3)   The type of the catch parameter is an interface that the exception type implements

There is no exact match for "FileNotFoundException" in our example. Based on the rules described above, the following entry will be the first match:

141

```
catch (IOException e) {
    System.out.println("I was here 2");
}
```

This is because "`FileNotFoundException`" is inherited from "`IOException`". **(see 2) above)**

As the "`finally`" block is guaranteed to be executed regardless of an exception being thrown or not, the output of the program is "`I was here 2`" followed by "`I was here 4`".

Q&A 34) What is the output of the following code? Select one correct answer.

```
public class TestLocalVar {
    private String var = "Hello World";
    public void printVar(){
        String var = "Hello everyone";      //1
        System.out.println(var);            //2
    }
    public static void main(String[] args){
        TestLocalVar obj = new TestLocalVar();
        obj.printVar();
    }
}
```

a. compilation error in line 1 as there is already a variable with the same name

b. compilation error in line 2 as the code is trying to access a private member

c. "`Hello World`"

d. "`Hello everyone`"

Correct answer: d.

a) is incorrect as there can be a local variable with the same name as an instance member.

b) is incorrect as the variable accessed at line 2 is the local variable var.

c) is incorrect as the method `printVar()` prints out the content of the local variable var and not the content of the instance variable var.

Q&A 35) What is the output of the following program? Select one correct answer.

```
public class MyClass {
    public static void main(String args[]) {
        int i = 1, r;
        r = r ^ i++;
        System.out.println(r);
    }
}
```

a.compilation error

b. 0

c. 1

d. 2

e. undefined

Correct answer: a.

The local variable r is used before being initialized.

Q&A 36) Which of the following are not valid lambda function definitions in Java? Select one answer.

a. `() -> System.out.println(this)`

b. `(String str) -> System.out.println(str)`

c. `str -> System.out.println(str)`

d. `(String s1, String s2) -> { return s2.length() - s1.length(); }`

e. `(s1, s2) -> s2.length() - s1.length()`

f. `() -> 8`

g. `() -> {9}`

h. `a -> System.out.println(str)`

i. `a,b -> a-b`

Correct answer: i.

The general syntax of the lambda functions in Java is:

`(arguments) -> {body}`

where arguments type can be either specified or not specified.

```
(arg1, arg2...) -> { body }

(type1 arg1, type2 arg2...) -> { body }
```

The curly brackets ("{", "}") can be omitted when the body of the function consists only of a single line of Java code.

When arguments type are not specified the compiler is able to infer tho information from the context where lambda function is defined/used.

`()  -> {  body  }` is also a valid lambda function with no arguments.

The option i. (`a,b -> a-b`) is the only one answer which does not meet any of these criteria.

Q&A 37) What is the output of the following code? Select one correct answer.

```
public class Car {
    private void accelerate() {
        System.out.println("Car accelerating");
    }
    private void break() {
        System.out.println("Car breaking");
    }
    public void control(boolean faster) {
        if (faster == true)
            accelerate();
        else
        break();
    }
    public static void main(String[] args){
```

```
        Car car = new Car();
        car.control(false);
    }
}
```

a. the code fails to compile

b. Car accelerating

c. Car breaking

d. no output

e. none of the above

Correct answer: a.

"break" is a reserved keyword and cannot be used for other purposes.

Q&A 38) What is the output of the following program? Select one correct answer.

```
public class MyClass {
    public static void main(String args[]) {
    int i = 2, r = 1;
    r = r++ ^ i++;
    System.out.println(r);
    }
}
```

a. compilation error

b. 0

146

c. 1

d. 2

e. 3

f. 4

Correct answer: e.

The expression `r = r++ ^ i++` contains operators with different precedence. Therefore, it is evaluated as follows:

- it evaluates first: `r ^ i (2 ^ 1 = 3)`

- then it increments `r` and `i`

- finally, the result obtained at 1) is assigned to variable `r`

Q&A 39) Which command line is the correct way of compiling a Java class? Select one correct answer.

```
a. java Test.java
```

```
b. java Test
```

```
c. javac Test.class
```

```
d. javac Test
```

```
e. javac Test.java
```

Correct answer: e.

The Java compiler is invoked by the javac command and it takes the filename including the .java extension.

Q&A 40) Which of the following are not Java primitive types? Select all that apply.

a. byte

b. short

c. integer

d. long

e. float

f. double

g. bool

h. char

Correct answer: c, g.

The valid list of Java primitive types is: `byte, short, int, long, float, double, boolean, char.`

Q&A 41) What is the output of the following program? Select one correct answer.

```
public class MyClass {
    public static void main(String args[]) {
        int i = 10;
        if (i++ % 10)
        {
            System.out.println("True");
        }
        else
        {
            System.out.println("False");
        }
    }
}
```

a. compilation error

b. "True"

c. "False"

d. runtime exception

Correct answer: a.

The condition i++ % 10 doesn't evaluate to boolean or Boolean. This will cause a compilation error.

Q&A 42) What is wrong with the following array initialization? Select one correct answer.

```
class ArrayTest {
    public static void main(String[] args) {
        // declares an array of integers
        int[] arr;
```

```
        arr[0]  =  1;
        arr[1]  =  2;
        arr[2]  =  3;
        arr[3]  =  4;
    }
}
```

a. `arr` length is not specified in the array variable declaration

b. `arr` is only declared but never created

c. the correct syntax for an array declaration is "`int arr[];`", not "`int[] arr;`"

d. none of the above

Correct answer: b.

If the initialization is done after the declaration (not in the same line like `int[] arr = { 1, 2, 3, 4};`), then we need to allocate memory for the elements of the array.

To accomplish this, we could change the first line to:

`int[] arr = new int[];`

Q&A 43) Which of the following constructs are infinite "`while`" loops? Choose all that apply.

a. `while(1) {};`

b. `while(true);`

```
c. while(true) {};
```

```
d. while(10 % 2);
```

```
e. while(1==1){}
```

```
f. while(1 & 1);
```

```
g. while(1 && 1);
```

Correct answer: b, e.

a, d, f are not correct as the `while` condition needs to evaluate to `boolean` or `Boolean`.

c is not correct as the "`;`" is detected by the compiler as not reachable.

g is not correct as operator "`&&`" can only be used with `boolean` (or `Boolean`) operands.

Q&A 44) What happens when the following code is compiled and run? Select one correct answer.

```
public class TestClass {
    private static String hello = "Hello world";
    public static void main(String args){
        System.out.println(hello.length());
    }
}
```

a. compilation error

b. runtime error

c. it will display: 11

d. it will display: 12

e. code is executed but no output is produced

Correct answer: b.

The signature for "main" method is incorrect. The program will compile fine but will fail to execute as a correct main entry point is not found.

Q&A 45) Given the code below, what is the reference count for the object created at line // 1   when the program execution is reaching the   line System.out.println("Here")? Select one correct answer.

```
class MyClass {
    public int val = 5;
    void displayVal(MyClass c) {
        System.out.println(c.val);
        System.out.println("Here");   // <- what
is the reference count for "obj" here?
    }
    public static void main(String[] args)
    {
        MyClass obj = new MyClass(); // 1
        obj.displayVal(obj);
    }
}
```

a. 0

b. 1

c. 2

d. cannot be determined

Correct answer: c.

When an object reference is passed to a method, a new object reference is created. Therefore when the code inside displayVal is executed there will be two references pointing to the original object "obj".

First reference is created when obj is created (MyClass obj = new MyClass();). The second reference is created by obj.displayVal(obj).

Hence the reference count will be 2 when line System.out.println("Here") is executed.

Q&A 46) Which of the following statements are true? Choose all that apply.

```
class Base {
    public int data = 0;

    void setData(int data) {
        this.data = data;
    }
}
class Derived extends Base {
    final void setData(int data) {          // 1
        this.data = data;                    // 2
```

153

```
        }
}
```

a. the code above will produce no compilation errors

b. the compiler will complain at line //1 because it tries to override a final method

c. the compiler will complain at line //2 because "data" is not a member of class "Derived"

d. class "Derived" cannot be inherited because it contains a final method

e. class "Derived" cannot be instantiated because it contains a final method

f. method "setData" cannot be overridden in any classes inherited from class "Derived"

Correct answer: a, f.

The effect of using "final" is that setData method from Derived class cannot be overridden in classes that inherit from Derived. But setData from the Base class can be overridden in any class that inherits from Base (as the method setData is not defined as final in this class).

Also, as any member of the Base class is also a member of the Derived class, the construct this.data = data is permitted and it will not generate a compilation error.

Q&A 47) Which of the following operators is not an arithmetic operator? Select one correct answer.

a. +

b. -

c. &

d. *

e. /

f. %

Correct answer: c.

& is the Bitwise AND operator.

The following are the arithmetic operators in Java:

+   Additive operator (also used for String concatenation)

-   Subtraction operator

*   Multiplication operator

/   Division operator

%   Remainder operator

Q&A 48) What is the output of the following Java program assuming that the file "data.txt" does not exist in the current folder? Select one correct answer.

155

```
import java.io.*;
public class MyClass {
    public void MyMethod() {
        try {
            FileInputStream input = new
FileInputStream("data.txt");
            input.close();
            }
        catch (IOException e) {
            System.out.println("I was here 1");
        }
        catch(Exception e) {
            System.out.println("I was here 2");
        }
    }
    public static void main(String args[]) {
        new MyClass().MyMethod();
    }
}
```

a. it displays "I was here 1"

b. it displays "I was here 2"

c. it displays "I was here 1" followed by "I was here 2"

d. nothing will be displayed

Correct answer: c.

The constructor FileInputStream ("data.txt") creates a FileInputStream by opening a connection to data.txt. As the file "data.txt" does not exist, a FileNotFoundException is thrown. FileNotFoundException inherits from IOException, therefore the exception is caught by the first catch block and the program will print "I was here 1".

Q&A 49) What happens when the following code is compiled and run? Select one correct answer.

```
public class TestClass {
    private static String hello = "Hello world";
    public static void main(String... params){
        System.out.println(hello.length());
    }
}
```

a. compilation error

b. runtime error

c. it will display: 11

d. it will display: 12

e. code is executed but no output is produced

Correct answer: c.

The signature of the main method is correct. Java accepts the definition of the main method parameter as a variable argument. The argument name is "params" which is acceptable. Using "args" as the name of the main method argument is common practice rather than mandatory requirement.

The code is syntactically correct and it prints the length of the String variable hello which is 11.

Q&A 50) Which of the following are not valid Java operators? Choose all that apply.

```
a. %
```

```
b. <>
```

```
c. <<
```

```
d. $
```

```
e. ++
```

```
f. #
```

```
g. ~
```

```
h. instanceof
```

Correct answer: b, d, f.

Here is a summery of all Java operators:

Simple Assignment Operator

=   Simple assignment operator

Arithmetic Operators

+   Additive operator (also used for String concatenation)

-      Subtraction operator

*   Multiplication operator

/   Division operator

%   Remainder operator

Unary Operators

+   Unary plus operator; indicates positive value (numbers are positive without this, however)

-    Unary minus operator; negates an expression

++   Increment operator; increments a value by 1

--   Decrement operator; decrements a value by 1

!   Logical complement operator; inverts the value of a boolean

Equality and Relational Operators

==   Equal to

!=   Not equal to

>   Greater than

>=   Greater than or equal to

<   Less than

<=   Less than or equal to

Conditional Operators

&&   Conditional-AND

|| Conditional-OR

?:   Ternary (shorthand for if-then-else statement)

Type Comparison Operator

instanceof   Compares an object to a specified type

Bitwise and Bit Shift Operators

~   Unary bitwise complement

<<   Signed left shift

>>   Signed right shift

>>>   Unsigned right shift

&   Bitwise AND

^   Bitwise exclusive OR

| Bitwise inclusive OR

Q&A 51) What will be the output of the following program? Select one correct answer.

```
class MyClass {
    public int val = 5;
    void change(int a, MyClass c) {
        c.val = 10;
        a = 20;
    }
    public static void main(String[] args)
    {
```

160

```
        MyClass obj = new MyClass();
        obj.change(obj.val, obj);
        System.out.println(obj.val);
    }
}
```

a. error

b. 5

c. 10

d. 20

Correct answer: c.

When calling `change(int a, MyClass c)` the first argument (a) will be passed by value. This means that "a = 20" statement inside of this method will not result in any changes for the obj.val passed in.

However for the second argument (c) the actual reference of obj will be passed in. So the statement "c.val = 10" will actually change the original value of `obj.val`.

Therefore, the value of `obj.val` after exiting the change method will be 10.

Q&A 52) Given the following program, select the correct statements. Select one answer.

```
package packageA;
class ClassA {
```

```
     public String memberA;
}
package packageB;
import packageA.ClassA;
public class ClassB{
}
```

a. it will print null

b. it will not print anything as memberA was not initialised

c. it will not compile

d. it will compile but it will throw an exception at runtime

Correct answer: c.

The code will not compile because ClassA is only visible inside packageA (the class has no access modifier, therefore it is visible only at package level). To make it visible outside its package the "public" access modifier needs to be used.

Q&A 53) Which of the following represent incorrect variable initializations in Java. Choose all that apply.

a. int val = 25;

b. int val = 025;

c. int val = a10;

d. int val = 0x27;

```
e. int val = 0b10010;

f. long longer = 999_99_9999L;

g. int val = 27hex;
```

Correct answer: c, g.

a. 25 is a correct representation of an integer using the decimal system.

b. 025 is a correct representation of an integer using the octal system.

d. 0x27 is a correct representation of an integer using the hexadecimal system (0x27 in hexadecimal is 39 in decimal).

e. is a correct representation of an integer using the binary system (18 in decimal).

f. is correct as (starting from Java SE7) Java allows any number of underscores characters (_) to appear between digits in a numerical literal.

c. is incorrect as "a" is not a valid digit for a number represented using the decimal system. It is only valid for a hexadecimal representation, but the this requires the "0x" or "0X" prefix.

g. is incorrect as the "hex" construct is not valid for any representation of an integer.

Q&A 54) What is the output of the following program? Select one answer.

```
public class MyClass {
    public static void main(String args[]) {
        int a = 3, b = 2, c = 0;
        int r;
        r = ++a + 1 * b << 4 - 3*c;
        System.out.println(r);
    }
}
```

a. 0

b. 96

c. 100

d. the code will fail to compile

Correct answer: c.

In terms of Java operator precedence, ++a has the highest precedence, followed by *, then followed by + and −. The lowest precedence is for the << operator. For arithmetic operators with same precedence the evaluation is performed from left to right

Given the above the the expression ++a + 1 * b << 4 − 3*c will evaluate as follows:

++3 + 1*2 << 4 − 3*0

4 + 1*2 << 4 − 3*0

4 + 2 << 4 − 0

6 << 4 which is 96

Q&A 55) Which of the following represent correct array initializations? Choose all that apply.

a. `int[] arr = { 1, 2, 3, 4};`

b. `int[4] arr = { 1, 2, 3, 4};`

c. `int[] arr = [ 1, 2, 3, 4];`

d. `int[] arr = { {1}, {2}, {3}, {4}};`

e. `int[][] arr = { {1}, {2}, {3}, {4}};`

Correct answer: a, e.

b. is not correct because we can never specify the size of an array on the left hand side of the "=" sign.

c. is not correct because a one-dimensional array can be initialized using a pair of braces ({}) and not [].

d. is not correct because two sets of "{}" are required to declare and initialize a bi-dimensional array.

a. and e. represent correct initializations of one-dimensional and multi-dimensional arrays.

Q&A 56) Which of the following represents a correct way of writing an infinite "do-while" loop? Choose all that apply.

a. `do {} while(1);`

b. do {} while(true);

c. do {} while(10 % 2);

d. do {} while(1==1);

e. do {} while(1 & 1);

f. do {} while(1 && 1);

Correct answer: b, d.

a, c, e are not correct as the while condition must to evaluate to boolean.

f is not correct as the "&&" operator is not applicable for integers.

Q&A 57) Which statements are true regarding the following Java class? Select one correct answer.

```
public class Foo {
        private int a,b,c;
        Foo (int a, int b, int c) {
            this.a = a;
            this.b = b;
            this.c = c;
        }
        Foo (int c, int d) {        // 1
            this(c,d,1);        // 2
        }
        Foo (int a, int b) {        // 3
            this.a = a;
```

166

```
            this.b = b;
            this.c = 1;
        }
}
```

a. the construct this(c, d, 1) is not valid

b. the second and the constructors are duplicated

c. the code will not compile as the default constructor is missing

d. the code will not generate any compilation errors

Correct answer: b.

Two constructors cannot have the same signature even if their implementation is different.

Q&A 58) What is the output of the following program? Select one correct answer.

```
class Base {
    public int data = 0;
    void setData(int data) {
        System.out.println("Base class called");
        this.data = data;
    }
}
class Derived extends Base {
    boolean setData(int newData) {
        System.out.println("Derived class
called");
        this.data = newData;
        return true;
```

```
    }
}
class MyClass {
    public static void main(String[] args)
    {
        Derived obj = new Derived();
        obj.setData(5);
    }
}
```

a. the code will fail to compile because "setData" of the Derived class does not return the same type as "setData" of the Base class

b. will display "Base class called"

c. will display "Derived class called"

d. will display "Derived class called" followed by "Base class called"

Correct answer: a.

Method signatures are taken into account when a method is overridden. The return type is not part of the method signature but, if the return type of method defined in the base class is a primitive type, then the same type must be returned by the overridden method.

In this example, the method "void setData(int data)" of the Base class has the same signature as "boolean setData(int newData)" of the Derived class. They qualify for overriding, but the return type is different so the compiler will produce an error.

Q&A 59) What is the output of the following program? Select one correct answer.

```
class AException extends Exception {}
class BException extends AException {}
class CException extends BException {}

public class MyClass {
    public void Method() {
        try {
            throw new CException();
        }
        catch(BException e) {              // 1
            System.out.println("Caught
BException");
        }
        catch(Exception e) {              // 2
            System.out.println("Caught
Exception");
        }
        catch(CException e) {
            System.out.println("Caught
CException");    // 3
        }
    }
    public static void main(String args[]) {
        new MyClass().Method();
    }
}
```

a. it will display "Caught BException"

b. it will display "Caught Exception"

c. it will display "Caught CException"

d. the code will fail to compile

Correct answer: d.

If there is an inheritance relationship between the caught exceptions, the exception of the base class cannot be caught before the exception of the derived class. In our example CException inherits from both BException and Exception and therefore exceptions of this class cannot be caught after exceptions of BException and Exception classes. This will result in a compilation error.

Q&A 60) We want the instance variable myTest to be accessible only to classes and interfaces defined in the same package. Which of the following declarations should be used? Select one correct answer.

a. private String myTest;

b. protected String myTest;

c. default String myTest;

d. String myTest;

e. public String myTest;

Correct answer: d.

The members defined without any access modifier have default accessibility (package accessibility). They are only accessible to classes and interfaces defined in the same package.

Q&A 61) What is the output of the following program? Select one correct answer.

```
public class MyClass {
    public static void main(String args[]) {
        int var = 10;
        System.out.print(var++);
        System.out.println(++var);
    }
}
```

a. 1012

b. 1011

c. 1112

d. 1111

Correct answer: a.

```
public class MyClass {
    public static void main(String args[]){
        int var = 10;
        System.out.print(var++);        //1
        System.out.println(++var);      //2
    }
}
```

Line //1 uses the "++" operator in postfix notation. This means the expression is evaluated first then the variable "var" is incremented. Line //2 uses the "++" operator in prefix notation.

This means the variable "`var`" is incremented then the expression is evaluated.

The two lines of code are equivalent to:

```
System.out.print(var);
var = var + 1;
var = var + 1;
System.out.println(var);
```

Q&A 62) Which statements are true regarding the following Java class? Choose all that apply.

```
public class MyClass {
    private int key;
    public int getKey () {                    // 1
            return (int) key;
    }
    public float getKey () {              // 2
                return (float) key;
    }
    public float getKey (float salt) { // 3
                return (float) key;
    }
}
```

a. method "`getKey()`" at //1 is correctly overloaded at //2

b. method "`getKey()`" at //2 is correctly overloaded at //3

c. the compiler will determine which "`getKey()`" method to use

d. the compiler will flag both line //1 and line //2 indicating that the two methods are duplicated.

Correct answer: b, d.

a. is incorrect as the return type is not part of the method signature and the compiler sees the two methods as identical.

b. is correct, "getKey()" method declared at line //2 is correctly overload at line //3, as the two methods have different signatures.

c. is incorrect - the compiler cannot detect which of the methods to call.

d. is correct - the compiler will flag the both method definitions as being duplicated.

Q&A 63) Which statements are true regarding the following Java program? Select one correct answer.

```java
public class Test {
    static int count;
    public void printCount(){
        System.out.print(count+ " ");
        count ++;
    }
    public static void main(String[] args){
        Test myTest = new Test();
        myTest.printCount();
        Test yourTest = new Test();
        yourTest.printCount();
    }
}
```

a. it will not compile as a non static method cannot access static members

b. it will not compile because count is not initialized and the compiler only assigns default values to non initialized non static members

c. it will print 0 0

d. it will print 0 1

Correct answer: d.

a. is incorrect as a non static method can access static members.

b. is incorrect as the compiler initializes all non initialized static and non-static members of type int with 0.

c. is incorrect as the program will print 0 1. When printCount() is called for the first time, the current value (0) of the variable "count" is printed. Then "count" is incremented to 1. When printCount() is called the second time, the current value of the variable "count", which is 1, is printed. Then "count" is incremented once again.

Q&A 64) Which of the following represents invalid String initializations in Java? Choose all that apply.

a. String s = "1abcde";

b. String s = "ab"c"de";

c. String s = "abc'd'e";

d. String s = "abc\tde";

e. String s = "abc\gde";

Correct answer: b, e.

a, b and d are valid String initializations.

b. is incorrect as the second set of " will mark the end of the string and the compiler will expect ; to finish the statement.

e. is incorrect as \g is not a valid escape sequence. Here is the list of value escape sequences in Java:

\t   Insert a tab in the text at this point.

\b   Insert a backspace in the text at this point.

\n   Insert a newline in the text at this point.

\r   Insert a carriage return in the text at this point.

\f   Insert a formfeed in the text at this point.

\'   Insert a single quote character in the text at this point.

\"   Insert a double quote character in the text at this point.

\\   Insert a backslash character in the text at this point.

Q&A 65) What will the following program display? Select one correct answer.

```
public class MyClass {
    public static void main(String args[]) {
        int var = 10;
        System.out.print(++var);
```

175

```
        System.out.println(var++);
    }
}
```

a. 1012

b. 1011

c. 1112

d. 1111

Correct answer: d.

```
public class MyClass {
    public static void main(String args[]) {
        int var = 10;
        System.out.print(++var);     //1
        System.out.println(var++);   //2
    }
}
```

Line 1 uses the "++" operator in prefix notation. This means the variable "var" is incremented first then the expression is evaluated. Line 2 uses the "++" operator in postfix notation. This means the expression is evaluated first, then the variable "var" is incremented.

The two lines of code are equivalent to:

```
    var = var + 1;
    System.out.print(var);
    System.out.println(var);
    var = var + 1;
```

Q&A 66) What is the output of the following Java code? Choose all that apply.

```
int intArrayOne[] = {200, 1, 10, 50};
int intArrayTwo[] = new int[2];
intArrayTwo[0] = 300;
System.arraycopy(intArrayOne, 2, intArrayTwo, 1,
1);
for (int i:intArrayTwo){
    System.out.print(i + " ");
}
```

a) 200 1 10 50 100

b) 200 300

c) 10

d) 10 50

e) 300

f) 300 10

Correct answer: f.

The line `intArrayTwo[0] = 300` makes the first element of the array 300. Then 10 is copied into the array using the `arraycopy()` method.

Q&A 67) What is the output of the following program? Select one answer.

```
class ForTest {
    public static void main(String[] args){
        for(int i=1, j=1; i<3 && j<=3; i++, +
+j){
            System.out.print( i + j);
        }
    }
}
```

a. 23

b. nothing will be displayed

c. 24

d. 235

e. 246

Correct answer: c.

The loop will be executed twice: first time for i=j=1 and it will display 2, and second time for i=j=2 and it will display 4. After the second step, j becomes 3. The expression i<3 && j<=3 is evaluated to false and the for loop completes its execution.

Q&A 68) Given the following Java program, select the correct statements? Select one correct answer.

```
public class MyClass {
    public static int count;
    void incCount(int step) {
        this.count += step;                  // 1
    }
```

```
public static void main(String[] args) {
    MyClass c = new MyClass();
    MyClass.count = 0;
    c.count ++;                          // 2
    MyClass.count++;                     // 3
    c.incCount(2);
    System.out.println(MyClass.count);
}
}
```

a. compilation error at line //1

b. compilation error at line //2

c. compilation error at line //3

d. the program will display 2

e. the program will display 3

f. the program will display 4

Correct answer: f.

Static members can be accessed using the name of the class (MyClass.count++) as well as using the name of the object reference variable (c.count++). Because of the second statement, accessing a static member using the "this" operator is also allowed.

Therefore, no compiler error will be generated, although the second option is not seen as good coding practice as it obscures the fact that "count" is a class variable.

In the program above "count" starts with the value of 0, then it is incremented first in line // 2 then second time in line // 3. Finally "count" is incremented by 2 (c.incCount(2)). Therefore, the value displayed by the program will be 4.

Q&A 69) What is the output of the following program? Select one correct answer.

```
class Base {
    void aMethod() {
        System.out.println("Method in Base class
called");
    }
}
class Derived extends Base {
    void aMethod() {
        System.out.println("Method in Derived
class called");
    }
}
class MyClass {
    public static void main(String[] args)
    {
        Base obj1 = new Derived();
        Derived obj2 = new Derived();
        obj1.aMethod();
        obj2.aMethod();
        obj1 = obj2;
        obj1.aMethod();
    }
}
```

a. compilation error

b. it will display:

```
Method in Derived class called
```

```
Method in Derived class called
```

```
Method in Derived class called
```

c. it will display:

```
Method in Base class called
```

```
Method in Derived class called
```

```
Method in Base class called
```

d. it will display:

```
Method in Base class called
```

```
Method in Derived class called
```

```
Method in Derived class called
```

Correct answer: b.

When resolving what object method to call then it is the instantiated class that matters rather than the reference type. In this example, both objects are created as "new Derived()" therefore the three calls to aMethod will invoke the method implementation from class Derived.

Q&A 70) Given the following Java program, specify which statements below are true. Select one correct answer.

```
public class MyClass {
    public void MyMethod() {            // 1
```

181

```
        throw new Exception();           // 2
        catch (Exception e) {            // 3
            throw new Exception();
        }
    }
    public static void main(String args[]) {
        new MyClass().MyMethod();        // 4
    }
}
```

a. compilation error at // 1 because MyMethod definition has no "throws" clause

b. compilation error at // 2 because Exception is an abstract class and cannot be instantiated

c. compilation error at // 3 because catch must have a corresponding try block

d. compilation error at // 4 because MyMethod call must be enclosed within a try-catch block

Correct answer: c.

"catch" cannot exist without a corresponding "try" block.

Q&A 71) MyClass and YourClass are two classes defined in the package com.oca. Which of the following are valid constructs inside YourClass? Choose all that apply.

a. import com.oca.MyClass*;

b. import com.MyClass;

c. import static com.oca.MyClass.*;

d. static import com.oca.MyClass.*;

e. import java.lang.*;

f. import com.oca.MyClass;

Correct answer: c, e, f.

a. is incorrect as "*" cannot be used to partially replace the name of a class in an import statement. "*" can only be used to replace the full class name (as in import java.lang.*, which will import the package java.lang and its members).

b. is incorrect as MyClass is not defined in the package com. It is defined in the package com.oca.

c. "static import" is not a valid statement. The correct way of importing stating members of a class is by using the "import static" statement. The order of the keywords import and static cannot be reversed.

Q&A 72) What will be the output of the following program? Select one correct answer.

```
public class MyClass {
    public static void main(String args[]) {
        String s = "abc\tde";
        System.out.println(s);
    }
}
```

a. compilation error

b. abcde

c. abc

d. de

e. abc   de

f. nothing will be displayed

Correct answer: e.

\t represents the escape character for TAB. Hence the following string will be displayed: abc   de.

Q&A 73) Which of the following are not Java unary operators? Select one correct answer.

a. +

b. -

c. ++

d. &&

e. !

f. ^

Correct answer: f.

See below the list of unary operators in Java:

+   Unary plus operator; indicates positive value (numbers are positive without this, however)

-     Unary minus operator; negates an expression

++   Increment operator; increments a value by 1

--   Decrement operator; decrements a value by 1

!   Logical complement operator; inverts the value of a boolean

Q&A 74) What is the output of the following program? Select one correct answer.

```
public class MyClass {
    public static void main(String args[]) {
        int arr[] = new int[5];
        for (int i=0; i<5; i++)
            arr[i] = 5-i;
            System.out.println(arr[arr.length]);
// 1
    }
}
```

a. 0

b. 1

c. compilation error at line // 1 as "length" is a method and has to be invoked as arr.length()

d. runtime exception at line // 1

Correct answer: d.

Using "`arr.length`" is correct as length is a property (public member) that stores the number of elements in the array. In this case length is 5.Therefore line //1 will try to display `arr[5]`, but `arr[5]` will throw a `java.lang.ArrayIndexOutOfBoundsException` as 0,1,2,3 and 4 are the valid indexes for an array of length 5.

Q&A 75) Which of the following blocks of code will produce this output? Select one correct answer.

```
1

2 2

3 3 3

4 4 4 4

5 5 5 5 5
```


a.
```
for(int x=1;x<=5;x++){
      for(int y=1;y<x;++y)
            System.out.print(y + " ");
   System.out.println("");
 }
```

b.

```
for(int x=1;x<=5;x++){
    for(int y=1;y<=x;++y)
        System.out.print(y + " ");
  System.out.println("");
 }
```

c.

```
for(int x=1;x<=5;x++){
    for(int y=1;y<=x;++y)
        System.out.print(x + " ");
  System.out.println("");
 }
```

d.

```
for(int x=1;x<=5;x++){
    for(int y=1;y<x;++y)
        System.out.print(x + " ");
  System.out.println("");
 }
```

Correct answer: c.

a) will display:

1

1 2

1 2 3

1 2 3 4

b) will display:

1

1 2

1 2 3

1 2 3 4

1 2 3 4 5

d) will display:

2

3 3

4 4 4

5 5 5 5

Q&A 76) What is the output of the following code? Select one correct answer.

```
package package1;
public class ClassP1 {}

package package1.package11;
public class ClassP11 {}

package package1.package12;
public class ClassP12 {}

package package2;
import package1.*;
public class ClassP2 {
    public static void main(String[] args){
        ClassP1 objP1;
        ClassP11 objP11;
```

```
        ClassP12 objP12;
    }
}
```

a. no output is produced

b. the code fails to compile

c. the code compiles but an exception is thrown at runtime

d. null is printed three times

Correct answer: b.

The import statement "import package1.*" only imports the class ClassP1, it does not import any classes from package11 and package12. Therefore ClassP11 and ClassP12 are not visible in ClassP2 and the code will fail to compile.

Q&A 77) Which statements are correct regarding the following program? Select one correct answer.

```
public class MyClass {
    static int getFromList(int... values, int
position)
    {
        return values[position];
    }
    public static void main(String[] args)
    {
        int val = getFromList(0, 1, 2, 3, 4, 2);
        System.out.println(val);
    }
}
```

a. the program will display 2

b. the program will display 1

c. the program will fail to compile as "int... values" is not a valid Java construct

d. the program will fail to compile as "int... values" is not in the last in the list of arguments

Correct answer: d.

"int... values" is a valid construct and represents a variable argument. However the Java compiler mandates that only one such parameter should be present and it must be in the last position in the list.

A correct definition for the get FromList method is:

```
static int getFromList(int position , int...
values)
```

Q&A 78) Given the following code select which of the following of assignments of variables listed below are correct. Choose all that apply.

```
abstract class Base {
    abstract void doMethod1();
    abstract void doMethod2();
    abstract void doMethod3();
}
abstract class Derived1 extends Base {
```

190

```
       void doMethod1() {};
       void doMethod2() {};
}
class Derived2 extends Derived1 {
       void doMethod3() {};
}
class Derived3 extends Derived2 {
}
```

a. Base b = new Base();

b. Base b = new Derived1();

c. Derived1 d1 = new Derived1();

d. Base b = new Derived2();

e. Derived1 d1 = new Derived2();

f. Derived3 d3 = new Derived2();

Correct answer: d, e.

Classes Base and Derived1 are abstract classes and they cannot be instantiated. For this reason answers a,b and c are incorrect.

A reference variable of a derived class cannot be used to refer to an object of its base class. Derived3 inherits from Derived2 therefore f. is incorrect (d3 is a reference variable of Derived3 and cannot point to an object of Derived2, its base class).

Q&A 79) What changes are required in order to make the

191

following Java program to compile? Select one correct answer.

```
public class MyClass {
    public void MyMethod() {                          // 1
        try {
            throw new Exception();
        }
        catch (Exception e) {
            throw new Exception();                    // 2
        }
    }
    public static void main(String args[]){  // 3
        new MyClass().MyMethod();                      // 4
    }
}
```

a. add a "throws" statement at line // 1

b. add a "throws" statement at line // 1 and another one at line // 3

c. add a "throws" statement at line // 3

d. enclose the call of MyMethod() at line //4 within a try-catch block

Correct answer: b.

a. is incorrect because the main method calls a method that throws an exception and therefore the main method should either handle the exception (using a try-catch block) or specify the exception to be thrown in its signature.

c. is incorrect as the throws statement at line //3 is not enough to

192

make the program to compile. MyMethod() should either specify the exception to be thrown in its signature or should handle the exception by enclosing line //2 within a try-catch block.

d. is incorrect as this is not enough to make the program to compile. Even if the call is enclosed within a try-catch, MyMethod() doesn't handle (using a try-catch block) nor specify the exception to be thrown in its signature.

The code below will compile and run with no errors:

```
public class MyClass {
    public void MyMethod() throws Exception{// 1
        try {
            throw new Exception();
        }
        catch (Exception e) {
            throw new Exception();          // 2
        }
    }
    public static void main(String args[])
throws Exception {        // 3
        try {
            new MyClass().MyMethod();       // 4
        }
        catch (Exception e)
        {}
    }
}
```

Q&A 80) Which statement is true regarding the following Java program? Select one correct answer.

```
public interface Executable {        // 1
        void execute();
        void run();
```

```
}
class Runner {
        public void run(Executable e) {    // 2
                e.execute();
        }
}
public class MyClass {
        public static void main(String[] args) {
        Runner runner = new Runner();
        Runner.run(() ->
System.out.println("Hello there."));        // 3
    }
}
```

a. implements a correct lambda function in Java at line // 3

b. lambda function at line // 3 must also provide implementation for the "run" method from Executable interface

c. "run" method from class Runner clashes with "run" method from Interface Executable

d. a lambda function cannot be written at line // 3 because interface Executable defines more than one method

Correct answer: d.

Only interfaces containing one single method definition are suitable to be used in lambda functions. Interfaces with one method are also called "functional interfaces".

Q&A 81) What is the output of the following Java program? Select one correct answer.

```
class StringTest {
    public static void main(String[] args) {
        String s1 = "abc";
        String s2 = "abc";
        if (s1 == s2) {
            System.out.print("Equal ");
        }
        else
        {
            System.out.print("Not Equal ");
        }
        if (s1.equals(s2)) {
            System.out.println("Equal");
        }
        else
        {
            System.out.println("Not Equal");
        }
    }
}
```

a. Equal Equal

b. Equal Not Equal

c. Not Equal Equal

d. Not Equal Not Equal

Correct answer: a.

When two strings are created using the assignment operator, the objects are stored in a pool of String objects. Before creating a new String object, Java verifies if an object with similar content already exists. If an object with similar content already exists,

JRE will return the object reference for the existing String object in the pool.

In our example, the line `String s1 = "abc"` will create a new object in the pool as no String with the value "abc" is found. When the line `String s2 = "abc"` executes, no new String object is created, as an object with the value "abc" already exists. Therefore, s2 will refer to the same object as s1.

As s1 and s2 refer to the same object, `s1==s2` returns true.

The method "`equals`" is overridden in the String class and is used to compare the content of two strings. Therefore, `s1.equals(s2)` will return true, as s1 and s2 have the same content.

The code will print `Equal Equal` - answer a)

Q&A 82) Which usage represents a valid way to run the following code? Select one correct answer.

```
public class HelloWorld {
        public static void main(String[] args) {
            System.out.println("Hello world");
        }
}
```

a. javac HelloWorld

b. java HelloWorld

c. javac HelloWorld.java

d. java HelloWorld.class

Correct answer: b.

"javac" is used to compile Java source files and to convert them to bytecode whereas the "java" command executes class files created by a java compiler.

Therefore, the correct command line used to run the code is java HelloWorld (the code needs to be compiled beforehand and the Helloworld.class created using javac HelloWorld.java).

Q&A 83) What is the output of the following Java program? Select all that apply.

```java
class StringTest {
    public static void main(String[] args) {
        String s1 = "abc";
        String s2 = new String("abc");
        if (s1 == s2) {
            System.out.print("Equal ");
        }
        else
        {
            System.out.print("Not Equal ");
        }
        if (s1.equals(s2)) {
            System.out.println("Equal");
        }
        else
        {
            System.out.println("Not Equal");
        }
    }
}
```

a. Equal Equal

b. Equal Not Equal

c. Not Equal Equal

d. Not Equal Not Equal

Correct answer: c.

The two reference variables, s1 and s2 refer to two different objects (Strings created using the assignment operator are placed in a pool of Strings whereas Strings created using the operator new always refer to different objects).

"s1 == s2" will compare the object references and not the object values. As s1 and s2 refer to two different objects, the result of this comparison is false.

For s1.equals(s2), the object values as compared. Even though the two variables refer to different objects, they define the same values ("abc"). The result of the second comparison is true.

Therefore, the code will print Not Equal Equal and the correct answer is c.

Q&A 84) Which statement is correct regarding the following program? Select one correct answer.

```
public class MyClass {
    static int getFromList(int position , int...
values)       // 1
    {
```

```
        return values[position];
    }

    public static void main(String[] args)
    {
            int val = getFromList(5, 0, 1, 2, 3,
4);   // 2
            System.out.println(val);
    }
}
```

a. it displays 4

b. compilation error at line // 1

c. compilation error at line // 2

d. it throws `ArrayIndexOutOfBoundsException`

Correct answer: d.

The main method is passing 6 numbers to `getFromList` method: 5, 0, 1, 2, 3, 4. The first number, 5, represents the position in the list of integers {0, 1, 2, 3, 4}. However the index of the first element is 0, the index of the second element is 1 etc. The index of the last element is 4 and there is no element on position 5. When trying to access an element on a position that doesn't exist, an `ArrayIndexOutOf BoundsException` is thrown at runtime.

Q&A 85) What is the output of the following program? Select one correct answer.

```
abstract class Animal {
```

```
    public void saySomething() {
        System.out.print(" ");
    }
}
class Cat extends Animal {
    public void saySomething() {
        System.out.print("Meow ");
    }
}
class Dog extends Animal {
    public void saySomething() {
        System.out.print("Woof ");
    }
}
class MyClass {
    public static void main(String[] args)
    {
        Animal dog = new Dog();    // 1
        Cat cat = new Cat();       // 2
        dog.saySomething();        // 3
        cat.saySomething();        // 4
        dog = cat;                 // 5
        dog.saySomething();        // 6
    }
}
```

a. compilation error at line // 1

b. compilation error at line // 5

c. Woof Meow Meow

d. Meow Woof

e. Meow Meow

f. Woof Meow Woof

Correct answer: c.

`dog.saySomething()` at line // 3 in main will display "Woof" as the reference variable `dog` refers to an object of the class `Dog`.

`cat.saySomething()` at line // 4 line in main will display "Meow" as the reference variable `cat` refers to an object of the class `Cat`.

`dog.saySomething()` at line // 6 line in main will display "Meow" as the reference variable `dog` refers to an object of the class `Cat`.

Q&A 86) Examine the following code and select all the incorrect statements.

```
public class HelloWorld {
    public void sayHello() {
        System.out.println("Hello world");
    }
}
```

a. the code will compile

b. the code will fail to compile as `main` method is not defined

c. the code will fail to execute as `main` method is not defined

d. a default `main` method is provided by the compiler.

e. the code will execute but it will produce no output

Correct answer: b, d, e.

A java class does not necessarily need to contain a `main` method in order to compile successfully. Hence a) is a correct statement. A `main` method signature is however required to be found in order to execute (any) java program. So c) statement is also correct. All the other statements are incorrect.

Q&A 87) Which of the following represents correct Java initializations? Choose all that apply.

```
a. double d = 123.4;

b. double d = 123,4;

c. double d = 1.234e2;

d. double d = 123.4d;

e. double d = 123.4f;

f. double d = 1234;
```

Correct answer: a, c, d, e, f.

The floating point types (`float` and `double`) can also be expressed using E or e (for scientific notation), F or f (32-bit float literal) and D or d (64-bit double literal, which is the default and by convention is omitted).

Q&A 88) Given the following Java class definitions and object instantiations, which of the following "`instanceof`" evaluates to true? Choose all that apply.

```
class Parent {}
class Child extends Parent implements
MyInterface {}
interface MyInterface {}
...
Parent obj1 = new Parent();
Parent obj2 = new Child();
```

a. obj1 instanceof Parent

b. obj1 instanceof Child

c. obj1 instanceof MyInterface

d. obj2 instanceof Parent

e. obj2 instanceof Child

f. obj2 instanceof MyInterface

Correct answer: a, d, e, f.

"instanceof" operator can be used to test if an object is an instance of a class, an instance of a subclass, or an instance of a class that implements a particular interface.

b. and c. are incorrect as the instance variable obj1 refers to on object of the class Parent.

Q&A 89) Which of the following statements are true for the following code? Choose all that apply.

```
String myArray[][] = new String[][] {null, {"a",
"b"}, {"0", null}};
```

a. `myArray.length` is 3

b. `myArray[0].length` is 0

c. `myArray[1].length` is 2

d. `myArray[2][1]` is null

Correct answer: a, c, d.

`myArray` is a two-dimesional   array. A two-dimensional array can be seen as a collection of objects and each object is a one-dimensional array.

`myArray` is therefore composed of 3 one-dimensional arrays. The first array is null. The second element is {"a", "b"}. The third element is {"0", null}.

a. is correct as the length of `myArray` is 3.

b. is incorrect as the construct `myArray[0].length` will throw a `NullPointerException` at runtime. `myArray[0]` is null and JVM throws a `NullPointerException` when trying to access a method or a variable with a null value.

c. is correct as the second element of `myArray` is a one-dimensional array of length 2.

d. is correct as `myArray[1][0]` refers to the second element of the array {"0", null} which is null.

Q&A 90) Which options are correct equivalents of a following "`while`" loop? Select all that apply.

```
int x=0;
do{
  System.out.println(x);
  x++;
 }while(x<10);
```

a.

```
int x=0;
while (x<10) {
       System.out.println(x);
       x++;
}
```

b.

```
int x=0;
while (x<=10) {
       System.out.println(x);
       x++;
}
```

c.

```
int x=0;
while (x<10) {
  System.out.println(x++);
}
```

d.

```
int x=0;
for (x=0; x<=10; x++) {
       System.out.println(x);
}
```

Correct answer: a, c.

b and d will have 11 iterations whereas the original loop has only 10 iterations. So b and d are incorrect. a, c are functionally equivalent with the original loop.

Q&A 91) What statement is true regarding the following class? Select one correct answer.

```
public class MyClass {
    private final int data;
    MyClass(int data) {
        this.data = data;
    }
    public String toString() {
        return "MyClass with data " + data;
    }
}
```

a. this class is a correctly implemented immutable Java class

b. declaring the class as "`final public class MyClass`", `MyClass` becomes a correctly implemented mutable class

c. in order for the above to be an immutable class it needs a getter method for the "`data`" field

d. both b. and c. above are true.

Correct answer: b.

Because MyClass is not a final class, it can be extended. New methods that modify the state of the object ("data" field in this particular example) can be added.

All the other criteria of an immutable class are met:

-   "data" is private and final

-   there are no methods that change the "data" field

Hence the correct answer is b.

Q&A 92) What is the correct way of calling the superclass constructor in a class hierarchy? Choose all that apply.

```
class MyBase {
    MyBase() {};
}
```

a.
```
class MyDerived extends MyBase {
    MyDerived() {
          super();
    }
}
```

b.
```
class MyDerived extends MyBase {
    MyDerived() {
          this();
    }
}
```

c.
```
class MyDerived extends MyBase {
    MyDerived() {
```

```
            MyBase();
    }
}
```

d.
```
class MyDerived extends MyBase {
    MyDerived() {
        MyBase.MyBase();
    }
}
```

e. `MyBase` class constructor cannot be called from `MyDerived` class constructor

f. `MyBase` class constructor is invoked automatically when `MyDerived` class constructor is called

Correct answer: a, f.

a - is correct. "`super`" can be used to invoke a method/constructor of the superclass.

b - is incorrect. "`this`" always points to an object's own instance.

c - is incorrect. "`MyBase();`" is not a syntactically correct invocation of the superclass constructor.

d - is incorrect. "`MyBase.MyBase();`" is not a syntactically correct invocation of the superclass constructor.

e - is incorrect. `MyBase` class constructor can be called from `MyDerived` class constructor.

f - is correct. If there is no explicit call to a superclass's constructor, a call to `super()` is inserted automatically by the compiler.

Q&A 93) Which statement is true regarding the following Java program, assuming the file test.txt doesn't exist in the working folder before running the code? Select one correct answer.

```
import java.io.File;
import java.io.FileReader;
public class MyClass {
   public void MyMethod() {
       try {
          File file = new File("test.txt");
          FileReader fileReader = new
FileReader(file);
       } catch (Exception e) {
       System.out.println("Exception reading
file: " + file.toString());             //1
     } finally {
     System.out.println("Done with file: " +
file.toString());                        //2
    }
 }

    public static void main(String args[]) {
        new MyClass().MyMethod();       // 3
        System.out.println("All good");
    }
}
```

a. runtime error at // 1 because the program is attempting to use a file that doesn't exist

b. compilation error at line // 3 because `try-catch` is missing

c. compilation errors at lines // 1 and // 2 because variable `file` is not accessible

d. it will display "All good"

Correct answer: c.

Lines //1 and //2 will cause compiler errors as the scope of the variable "file" is limited to the "try" block in which this variable is defined. The variable "file" must be declared before "try" to make it visible in the "catch" and "finally" blocks.

Q&A 94) Examine the following code and select one correct answer.

```
public class HelloWorld {
    void sayHello();
    public static void main(String[] args) {
        System.out.println("Hello world");
    }
}
```

a. the code will not compile as there is no access modifier specified for the method "sayHello"

b. the code will not compile as the method "sayHello" is not implemented

c. the compiler will provide a default body for the method "sayHello"

d. the code will compile as "sayHello" is not invoked anywhere

Correct answer: b.

A method can be implemented by the class in which it is declared or by any of the derived classes (in which case the method must be declared as abstract).

As there is no implementation provided for the method "sayHello", the code will fail to compile. Adding an empty body to the sayHello() method will fix this problem. See below:

```
public class HelloWorld {
    void sayHello(){}

    public static void main(String[] args) {
        System.out.println("Hello world");
    }
}
```

Q&A 95) What will be the output of the following Java program? Select one correct answer.

```
class MyClass {
    public static void main(String[] args){
        int value1 = 2;
        int value2 = 2;
        if(value1 == value2)
            System.out.print("Here1 ");
            if(value1 != value2)
                System.out.print("Here2 ");
                if(value1 >= value2)
                    System.out.print("Here3 ");
                if(value1 < value2)
                    System.out.print("Here4 ");
                    if(value1 <= value2)
                        System.out.print("Here5");
    }
}
```

a. nothing will be displayed

b. Here 1

c. Here1 Here3 Here4

d. Here1 Here3 Here5

e. Here1 Here3 Here4 Here5

Correct answer: d.

Don't be mislead by the indentation here. The code is identical with the code below where the following if statements will be evaluated to true:

```
class MyClass {
    public static void main(String[] args){
        int value1 = 2;
        int value2 = 2;
        if(value1 == value2)          // true
            System.out.print("Here1 ");
        if(value1 != value2)
            System.out.print("Here2 ");
        if(value1 >= value2)          // true
            System.out.print("Here3 ");
        if(value1 < value2)
            System.out.print("Here4 ");
        if(value1 <= value2)          // true
            System.out.print("Here5 ");
    }
}
```

Q&A 96) Examine the following class and select all the correct answers.

```
class MyClass {
    private int data;
    private MyClass() {
        data = 0;
    }
    static void doStatic() {
        System.out.println("Static method
invoked!");
    }
}
```

a. compilation error because the only constructor of the class is declared `private`

b. compilation error because because a non static class cannot contain a `static` method

c. class `MyClass` cannot be instantiated

d. the default constructor is used when creating instances of `MyClass`

e. method `doStatic()` can be called using `MyClass.doStatic()`

Correct answer: c, e.

a) is incorrect as it is allowed to have private constructors. It is also allowed for non-static classes to contain static methods. Therefore, answer b) is also incorrect.

A class with all the constructors declared private cannot be instantiated. This is the case of the class in the example above. Once a constructor is specified (regardless of being "public" or "private") the compiler no longer generates a default (public) constructor. So answer c) above is correct and d) is incorrect.

Also static members/methods can be used even if the class cannot be instantiated. The static modifier removes any "ties" with any class instances. e) is therefore a correct answer.

Q&A 97) What is the output of the following program? Select one correct answer.

```
class MyClass   {
    @Override                          // 1
    public String toString() {
        super.toString();              // 2
          return "Hi there!";
    }
    public static void main(String[] args) {
        MyClass obj = new MyClass();
        System.out.println(obj.toString());
    }
}
```

a. compilation error at line // 1

b. compilation error at line // 2

c. Hi there!

d. runtime error

Correct answer: c.

The Object class (found in the java.lang package) is the base class of all the Java classes.

Even if a class does not explicitly extend another class it automatically extends the Object class.

In our example,

```
class MyClass  {
```

is equivalent to:

```
class MyClass  extends Object {
```

One of the methods defined in Object class is:

```
public String toString()
```

and trying to override this method in MyClass is perfectly legitimate.

To conclude, the program will compile and execute successfully and will output "Hi there!"

Q&A 98) Examine the following code and select one correct answer.

```
public class NestedVariables {
    int aVar = 3;                       // 1
    public static void main(String[] args) {
        int aVar = 4;                   // 2
        if (aVar == 4)
        {
            int aVar = 5;           // 3
            System.out.println(aVar);
```

```
        }
    }
}
```

a. compilation error at line // 1

b. compilation error at line // 2

c. compilation error at line // 3

d. it will print 3

e. it will print 4

f. it will print 5

Correct answer: c.

The code will fail to compile at line 3 as there is already a local variable called `aVar` (declared at line 2).

Q&A 99) Which of the following represents correct initialization in Java? Select one correct answer:

```
a.  float f = 123.4;

b.  float f = 123,4;

c.  float f = 1.234e2;

d.  float f = 123.4d;

e.  float f = 123.4f;
```

Correct answer: e.

A floating-point literal is of type `float` if it ends with the letter F or f; otherwise its type is double and it can optionally end with the letter D or d.

Q&A 100) What is the output of the following Java program? Select one answer.

```
class MyClass {
    public static void main(String[] args){
        int value1 = 2;
        int value2 = 2;
        if (value1 == value2)
            if (value2 == 3)
                value1++;
        else
            value2++;
        System.out.print(value1 + " ");
        System.out.println(value2);
    }
}
```

a. 2 2

b. 2 3

c. 3 2

d. 3 3

Correct answer: b.

217

Despite being aligned under the first "if", the "else" belongs to the second "if".

By fixing the indentation becomes obvious that "value2++" is executed before displaying the results.

```
class MyClass {
    public static void main(String[] args){
        int value1 = 2;
        int value2 = 2;
        if (value1 == value2)
            if (value2 == 3)
                value1++;
            else
                value2++;
        System.out.print(value1 + " ");
        System.out.println(value2);
    }
}
```

Q&A 101) What is the output of the following Java program? Select one answer.

```
public class MyClass {
    public static void main(String[] args) {
        int[][][] arr = { { { 1, 1, 1, 1 }, { 2,
2, 2, 2 } },
                { { 3, 3, 3 }, { 4, 4, 4 }, { 5,
5 } },
                { { 6, 6, 6 }, { 7, 7, 7 }, { 8,
8 }, { 9, 9, 9 } } };

        System.out.println(arr[1][2][1]);
    }
}
```

a. compilation error

b. `ArrayIndexOutOfBoundsException`

c. 5

d. 3

e. 6

Correct answer: c.

A multi-dimensional array is an array of arrays. In our example, each element of the array `arr` is also a bi-dimensional array:

`arr[0] = { { 1, 1, 1, 1 }, { 2, 2, 2, 2 } }`

`arr[1] = { 3, 3, 3 }, { 4, 4, 4 }, { 5, 5 } }`

`arr[2] = { { 6, 6, 6 }, { 7, 7, 7 }, { 8, 8 }, { 9, 9, 9 } }`

In `arr[1]`, the element of index 2 is also an array: {5, 5}. The element of index 1 in this array is 5.

To conclude, `arr[1][2][1]` is 5 and the program will print 5.

Q&A 102) Which of the following statements are correct regarding the "`break`" statement? Select all the correct answers:

a. "`break`" is used to exit the "`for`", "`for-each`", "`do`" and "`do-while`" loops

b. "break" is used to exit a method

c. "break" is used to exit a {...} delimited Java block of code

d. "break" is used exit a switch statement

e. "break" is used to skip a section of code delimited by the first "continue" statement.

Correct answer: a, d.

The break statement is used to exit (break out of) the "for", "for-each", "while" and "do-while" loops and the switch construct.

Q&A 103) What statements are true regarding the following Java class? Select one correct answer.

```
class MyClass {
    private int data;
    public MyClass() {
        data = 0;
    }

    public boolean MyClass(int data) {
        this.data = data;
        return true;
    }
}
```

a. class MyClass can be instantiated as follows: MyClass obj = new MyClass(3);

b. there will be a compilation error when defining "`public void MyClass(int data)`" saying that constructor cannot have a return value;

c. the following line is valid: "`boolean b = new MyClass().MyClass(4);`"

d. the class `MyClass` has two constructors

Correct answer: c.

By specifying a return value for a constructor this will cause Java compiler to treat it as a regular method rather than a class constructor. It will just be a method with an "unfortunate" name. The compiler will issue a warning but it will not prevent the user from doing this.

Although it may seem a bit confusing the following statement (answer c) is correct:

```
boolean b = new MyClass().MyClass(4);
```

This works as follows:

- "`new MyClass()`" will create a reference to a new instance of `MyClass` using the only class constructor

- the method `MyClass(4)` will be called for the new object created above

- the return value of `MyClass(4)` method will be assigned to variable b

To conclude, it is possible to define methods with the same name

221

as the class name, but it is discouraged and seen as bad coding practice.

Q&A 104) What is the output of the following program? Select one correct answer.

```java
class MyClass   {
    int data;
    MyClass(int data) {
        this.data = data;
     }
    public static void main(String[] args) {
        MyClass obj1 = new MyClass(4);
        MyClass obj2 = new MyClass(4);
        if (obj1 == obj2) {
            System.out.println("Objects are
equal ");
        }
        else {
            System.out.println("Objects are not
equal ");
        }
        if (obj1.equals(obj2)) {            // 1
            System.out.println("Objects are
equal ");
        }
        else {
            System.out.println("Objects are not
equal ");
        }
     }
}
```

a. compilation error at // 1 because "equals" method is not defined

b. "Objects are equal " followed by "Objects are equal"

c. "Objects are not equal " **followed by** "Objects are equal"

d. "Objects are not equal " **followed by** "Objects are not equal"

e. can't be determined for certain

Correct answer: d.

When the "==" operator is used, the two reference variables are compared. As obj1 and obj2 are two reference variables pointing to two different objects, the result of the comparison obj1 == obj2 is false.

Now about "equals" method: this method exists in the java.lang.Object class. Because all the classes inherit from the Object class, line //1 will not cause a compilation error.

The "equals" implementation from the Object class will be invoked because MyClass does not override this method. This implementation compares whether the two object variables refer to the same object. As obj1 and obj2 refer to two different objects, obj1.equals(obj2) will return false.

Q&A 105) Which of the following represent correct Java pre defined exception? Choose all that apply.

a. UnsupportedOperationException

b. RuntimeException

c. NullPointerException

d. `FloatingPointException`

e. `InvalidParameterException`

f. `ArrayIndexOutOfBoundsError`

g. `MethodNotDefinedException`

Correct answer: a, b, c, e.

FloatingPointException, ArrayIndexOutOfBoundsError and MethodNotDefinedException are not valid Java exceptions.

Q&A 106) Which statement is true regarding the following Java program? Select one correct answer.

```
public interface IntfA {
    int FooA(int a);
}
public interface IntfB {
    int FooB(String b);
}
public class MyClass {
    void MyMethod(IntfA i) {};
    void MyMethod(IntfB i) {};

public static void main(String[] args) {
    MyClass class = new MyClass();
    class.MyMethod((a) ->
System.out.println(a)); // 1
    }
}
```

a. it will call "`MyMethod(IntfA i)`"

b. it will call "MyMethod(IntfB i)"

c. it will call "MyMethod(IntfA i)" followed by "MyMethod(IntfB i)"

d. it will cause compilation error at line // 1

Correct answer: d.

In this example the compiler is not able infer the type of argument a from the lambda definition. Both "int" (because of the functional interface IntfA) or "String" (because of the functional interface IntfB) are equally good candidates and the compiler cannot make a decision. Hence specifying the argument type is a must in this particular case.

Q&A 107) Which of the following statements are correct? Choose all that apply.

a. "class" and "object" can be used interchangeably

b. an object is an instance of a class

c. a class is an instance of an object

d. users can define multiple instances of a class

e. objects have a lifespan but classes do not

Correct answer: b, d, e.

A `class` and an `object` are two different entities. A `class` represents a template used to specify the behaviour and properties of an `object`. An `object` is also referred to as an `instance` of a class.

A `class` can have multiple `instances`. An `instance` of a class (object) has a lifespan which starts from the moment the object is created and lasts until the object is no longer referenced by a variable or goes out of scope.

Q&A 108) What will the following program display? Select one correct answer.

```
class ConditionalTest {
    static boolean alwaysFalse() {
        System.out.print("3 ");
        return false;
    }
    public static void main(String[] args){
        int data = 1;
        if ((data == 2) && (alwaysFalse() ==
false))
            System.out.print("1 ");
        else
            System.out.print("2 ");
    }
}
```

a. 1

b 2

c. 3 1

d. 2 1

e. 1 3

f. 2 3

Correct answer: b.

To evaluate the expression (d a t a == 2) & &
(alwaysFalse() == false), the first condition, (data ==
2) is evaluated first. Because the value of variable data is 1,
(data == 2) evaluates to false. As a result, the second
condition (alwaysFalse() == false) will not be evaluated
and the entire expression is set to false.Therefore, only 2 will be
displayed.

Q&A 109) What statements are true regarding the following
Java class. Select one correct answer.

```
class MyClass {
    private int data = 0;                        // 1
    {
        data = 1;                                // 2
    }
    public  MyClass(int data) {
        this.data = data;
    }
    public int getData() {
        return data;
    }
    public static void main(String[] args)
    {
        MyClass obj = new MyClass(3);
        System.out.println(obj.getData());
    }
}
```

a. compilation error at line //1

b. 3

c. 1

d. compilation error at line // 2

Correct answer: b.

The syntax at line //1 is called "instance variable initializer" and the syntax at line //2 is called "initializer block" and they are valid Java constructs.

In term of initialization sequence the order is the following:

- instance variable initializers first

- followed by the initializer block(s)

- and lastly the code in the constructor.

Therefore for MyClass example the code in the constructor will be executed last so the data field will be ultimately set to value of 3.

Q&A 110) Given the following Java classes:

```
class MyBase {
}

class MyDerived1 extends MyBase {
```

```
}

class MyDerived2 extends MyBase {
}
```

And the following class instantiations:

```
MyBase b = new MyBase();

MyDerived1 d1 = new MyDerived1();

MyDerived2 d2 = new MyDerived2();
```

Which of the following statements return true? Choose all that apply.

a. d1 instanceof MyBase

b. d2 instanceof MyBase

c. d1 instanceof MyDerived2

d. b instanceof MyDerived1

e. d1 instanceof b

f. b instanceof d1

g. d2 instanceof d2

Correct answer: a, b.

First thing to note here is that the syntax of "instanceof" Java operator is:

```
<object_reference> instanceof <ClassType>
```

thus e,f and g are not syntactically correct and will result in compiler error.

Secondly, "`<object_reference> instanceof <ClassType>`"

is evaluated to true when <object_reference> is an instance of a <ClassType> or super classes of <ClassType>.

The only correct answers are: a. and b.

Q&A 111) Which of the following statements are accepted by the Java compiler? Choose all that apply.

a. `package com.mockexam.tests;`

b. `package com.mockexam.*;`

c. `package tests;`

d. `package 1;`

e. `package default;`

Correct answer: a, c.

*, default and 1 are not valid Java identifiers.

Q&A 112) What statements are true regarding the following Java program? Choose all that apply.

```
public class MyClass {
    public static void main(String[] args) {
        Float f1 = new Float(1);
        if (f1 > 0) {
            Float f2 = new Float(2);
            f2 = 3f;
        }
        System.out.println(f1);   // 1
    }
}
```

a. "f1" and "f2" are eligible for garbage collection when the program starts the execution of line // 1

b. "f2" is already garbaged collected when the program starts the execution of line // 1

c. "f2" is eligible for garbage collection when the program starts the execution of line // 1

d. "f2" is not visible when the program starts the execution of line // 1

Correct answer: c, d.

a. is not correct. f1 is not eligible for garbage collection as it is still used in the construct present at line //1.

b . f2 is out of scope and is therefore eligible for garbage collection. But as the garbage collector is controlled by the JVM one can never know when f2 will be garbage collected. Therefore b. is not correct.

c. is correct. As f2 is out of scope, it is also eligible for garbage collection.

d. is correct. The scope of variable f2 starts from the line where it is declared until the end of the if block.

Q&A 113) What is the output of the following Java program? Select one correct answer.

```
class ConditionalTest {
    static boolean alwaysFalse() {
        System.out.print("3 ");
        return false;
    }
    public static void main(String[] args){
        int data = 1;
        if ((data == 2) || (alwaysFalse() ==
false))
            System.out.print("1 ");
        else
            System.out.print("2 ");
    }
}
```

a. 1

b. 2

c. 3 1

d. 2 1

e. 1 3

f. 2 3

Correct answer: c.

To evaluate the expression `(data == 2) || (alwaysFalse() == false)`, the first condition, `(data==2)` is evaluated first. Because the value of variable data is 1, `(data==2)` will evaluate to false. To evaluate the second expression, `(alwaysFalse() == false)`, the method `alwaysFalse()` will be called. As a result, "3 " will be printed first. Because `alwaysFalse()` returns false, `(alwaysFalse() == false)` will be evaluated to true.

Therefore, `(data == 2) || (alwaysFalse() == false)` evaluates to true and "1 " will be printed as well.

Q&A 114) What is the output of the following Java program? Select one correct answer.

```
import java.util.ArrayList;
public class MyClass {
    public static void main(String[] args) {
        ArrayList<Integer> list = new
ArrayList<Integer>();
        list.add(0);
        list.add(1);
        list.add(1,2);
        list.add(3);
        System.out.println(list);
    }
}
```

a. `[0, 1, 2, 3]`

b. `[0, 2, 1, 3]`

c. `[3, 2, 1, 0]`

d. [3, 1, 2, 0]

Correct answer: b.

Using the add method, elements can be added at the end of the list or at a specified position:

add(E e) - inserts element "e" (of type E) at the end of the list.

add((int index, E e) - inserts element "e" (of type E) in position index; all the elements at or beyond the point of insertion are shifted up.

This how the elements are added to the list in the example above:

Operation	List
list.add(0)	[0]
list.add(1)	[0, 1]
list.add(1,2)	[0, 2, 1]
list.add(3)	[0, 2, 1, 3]

Q&A 115) What is the final value of "val" at the end of the "for" loop? Select one correct answer.

```
int val = 1;
for (int i = 0; i<10; i++) {
    if (i % 3 == 0)
        continue;
    val += i;
}
```

a. 1

b. 37

c. 28

d. 27

e. 46

Correct answer: c.

The statement "`val +=i`" (equivalent to "`val = val + i`") will be executed for the steps for which the reminder of i divided by 3 is not 0. If the reminder of i divided by 3 is 0, "`i % 3 == 0`" will evaluate to true. When "`i % 3 == 0`" evaluates to true the statements "`val += i`" is skipped. This is because continue exits the current iteration and starts the next iteration.

The statement `val +=i` is reached and executed for the following values of i: 0,1,2,4,5,7 and 8.

Therefore the final value of "`val`" will be:

1 (initial value) + 0 + 1 + 2 + 4 + 5 + 7 + 8 = 28

Q&A 116) Which statements are true regarding the following Java class? Select one correct answer.

```
class MyClass {
    private static int data = 0;
    public static void incrementData() {
```

```
        data++;
    }
    public void decrementData() {
        data--;                                  // 1
    }
    public static void main(String[] args)
    {
        MyClass obj = new MyClass();
        obj.incrementData();                     // 2
        MyClass.incrementData();
        MyClass.decrementData();                 // 3
        System.out.println(data);
    }
}
```

a. compilation error at line // 1 as "data" is accessed without class name (MyClass.data)

b. compilation error at line // 2 as static method incrementData() is invoked using an object

c. compilation error at line // 3 as non static method is invoked using class name

d. 0

e. 1

Correct answer: c.

The key aspect here is that static methods can be invoked either using class name or an object, whereas non static methods (a.k.a instance methods) can only be called using an object. Therefore, the construct MyClass.decrementData() is not correct as decrementData() is a non-static method and will produce a compilation error.

Q&A 117) Given the following Java class hierarchy:

```
class Base {
}

class Derived1 extends Base {
}

class Derived2 extends Base {
}
```

And the following class instantiations:

```
Base b = new Base();

Derived1 d1 = new Derived1();

Derived2 d2 = new Derived2();
```

Which of the following Java statements are correct? Select one correct answer.

a. b = d1;

b. d2 = b;

c. d1 = (Base)b;

d. d2 = d1;

e. d1 = (Derived1)d2;

Correct answer: a.

a. - is correct because we can assign a reference variable of a derived class to a reference variable of its base class.

b. - is incorrect because we cannot assign a reference variable of a base class to a reference variable of one of its derived classes.

c. - is incorrect for the same reason as b. Using a cast will not solve the problem.

d. - is incorrect because we cannot assign a reference variable of a derived class to a reference variable of another derived class.

e. - is incorrect for the same reason as d. Using cast will not solve the problem either.

Q&A 118) Which of the following statements regarding Java exceptions are true? Select all that apply.

a. "`finally`" block always executes

b. the order of the exceptions caught in the catch blocks is never important

c. a checked exception is a subclass of `java.lang.RuntimeException`

d. `java.lang.Throwable` is the base class of all exceptions

e. an exception can be re - thrown in the `catch` block

f. exceptions are divided into three categories: checked exceptions, runtime (or unchecked exceptions) and errors

Correct answer: a, d, e, f.

b) is not correct. The order does not matter for unrelated classes, but it is important for related classes. If the caught exceptions share an IS-A relationship, the base class exceptions cannot be caught before the derived class exceptions.

c) is false because by definition, a checked exception is a subclass of `java.lang.Exception`, but not a subclass of `java.lang.RuntimeException`. A subclass of `java.lang.RuntimeException` is an unchecked exception.

Q&A 119) Which of the following statements is correct? Select one correct answer.

```
package
this_is_a_very_long_package_name_for_1st_oracle_
exam;
```

a. package declaration is incorrect because it starts with a reserved keyword ("this")

b. package declaration is incorrect because it contains an invalid character ("_")

c. package definition is incorrect because it contains a digit ("1")

d. package definition is correct

e. Java compiler restricts the length of package names to 25 characters

f. Java compiler expects a package name in format:

"com.domain.package_name"

Correct answer: d.

A package name has to be a valid Java identifier.

A valid Java identifier has the following properties:

- unlimited length

- starts with a letter (a-z), a currency sign or an underscore

- can use a digit, but not in the first position

- can use an underscore in any position

- can use a currency sign in any position

The name in our package declaration complies with all the above rules.

Q&A 120) Given the following class and interface definitions, select all the expressions that evaluate to true.

```
class Parent {}

class Child extends Parent implements
MyInterface {}

interface MyInterface {}

class Cousin implements MyInterface{}
```

...

```
Parent parent = new Parent();

Child child = new Child();

Cousin cousin = new Cousin();
```

a. parent instanceof Object

b. MyInterface instanceof Object

c. Child instanceof Child

d. Child instanceof Parent

e. cousin instanceof Parent

f. child instanceof Parent

Correct answer: a, f.

b,c,d are syntactically incorrect as the operator instanceof requires a reference variable on the left hand side, not a class.

e will also cause a compilation error as there is no relationship between the reference variable cousin and the class Parent.

Q&A 121) Which statements are true regarding the following Java class? Select one correct answer.

```
class MyClass {
    private static int data = 0;
    public static void incrementData() {
        data++;
    }
    public void decrementData() {
        data--;                          // 1
    }
    public static void main(String[] args)
    {
            MyClass obj = new MyClass();
            obj.incrementData();         // 2
            MyClass.incrementData();
            obj.decrementData();
            System.out.println(data);
    }
}
```

a. compilation error at line // 1 as static member "data" is accessed without class name (MyClass.data)

b. compilation error at line // 2 as static method incrementData() is invoked using a reference variable

c. 0

d. 1

Correct answer: d.

Static methods can be accessed either using the name of an object reference variable or the name of the class. Both "obj.incrementData()" and "MyClass.incrementData()" are correct (although the first option is seen as bad coding practice). And because data is also declared as static all the operations are carried out against the same variable.

"data" starts with an initial value of 0 and is incremented twice and decremented once. This gives the result of 1.

Q&A 122) Examine the following Java program and select one correct answer.

```
public class NestedComments {
    public static void main(String[] args) {
/*
//              int aVar = 5;     // comment
 */
            System.out.println("Hello world!");

    }
}
```

a. the program will compile with no errors

b. the program will not compile as the compiler does not allow mixing end-of-line comments ("//") with multiline comments ("/* ... */")

c. the program will not compile as 2 end-of-line comments ("//") are present on the same line

d. the program will compile but it will also generate a warning about the use of nested comments in the code.

Correct answer: a.

Java compiler allows using end of line comments within a multiline comment.

Also two or more end-of-line comments are accepted on the same line. The commented area starts from the first occurrence of "//".

Q&A 123) Which objects are eligible for garbage collection when the code reaches line // 9 in the program below? Select one correct answer.

```
public class MyClass {
    public static void main(String[] args) {
        Float f1 = new Float(1);          // 1
        Float f2 = new Float(2);          // 2
        Float f3 = new Float(3);          // 3
        f1 = f2;                          // 4
        Float f11 = f1;                   // 5
        f1 = null;                        // 6
        f2 = null;                        // 7
        f3 = null;                        // 8
        System.out.println("Who's up for garbage
collection?");// 9
    }
}
```

a. object created at line //1

b. object created at line // 2

c. object created at line // 3

d. objects created at line // 1 and line // 2

e. objects created at line // 1 and line // 3

f. objects created at line // 2 and line // 3

g. none

Correct answer: e.

An object is eligible for garbage collection when it can no longer be accessed. This can happen when the object goes out of scope or when the object has no reference variable pointing to it (the reference count is 0).

Let's study the reference count for each of the three objects (f1, f2, f3) in our example. They all start with a reference count of 1 in lines // 1, // 2 and // 3.

We will refer to these three object as follows:

- "object1" the object created at line // 1

- "object2" the object created at line // 2

- "object3" the object created at line // 3

After the execution of line //3, the reference count is:

object1: 1   object2: 1   object3: 1

After the execution of line // 4 (f1 = f2), there will no reference variable pointing to object 1, but 2 reference variables, f1 and f2 will point to object 2.

Therefore, after line //4, the reference count is:

object1: 0   object2: 2   object3: 1

Next line: f11 = f1;

After the execution of line // 5, another reference variable, f11, will point to object 2. The reference count becomes:

object1: 0   object2: 3   object3: 1

After the execution of line // 6, the reference count of object 2 is decremented (f1 is a reference variable for object 2 and is assigned an explicit null):

object1: 0   object2: 2   object3: 1

After the execution of line // 7, the reference count of object 2 is decremented again:

object1: 0   object2: 1   object3: 1

After the execution of line //7, the reference count of object 3 is decremented (f3 is a reference variable for object 3 and is assigned an explicit null):

object1: 0   object2: 1   object3: 0

Therefore, when the code execution reached line // 9, the only object not eligible for garbage collection is object 2.

Q&A 124) What will the following program display? Select one correct answer.

```
class BitTest {
    public static void main(String[] args) {
        int bitmask = 0x000F;
        int val = 0x2222;
        System.out.println(val & bitmask << 4);
    }
}
```

a. nothing. Compilation error

b. nothing. Runtime error

c. 32

d. 16

e. 0x20

Correct answer: c.

To evaluate the expression `val & bitmask << 4` we first need to convert the hexadecimal numbers 0x000F and 0x2222 to binary numbers:

`0x2222 & 0x000F << 4` becomes `0010 0010 0010 0010 & 0000 0000 0000 1111 << 4.`

As the "<<" operator has higher precedence then the binary AND operator (&), bitmask << 4 will be evaluated first.

Therefore, the expression is evaluated as follows:

`0010 0010 0010 0010 & 0000 0000 0000 1111 << 4`

`0010 0010 0010 0010 & 0000 0000 1111 0000`

`0000 0000 0010 0000`

The decimal value of the binary number 0000 0000 0010 0000 is 32.

Q&A 125) What is the output of the following program? Select one correct answer.

```
public class MyClass {
    public static void main(String[] args) {
        Integer arr[] = new Integer[5];
        System.out.println(arr[0]);
    }
}
```

a. 0

b. null

c. unspecified

d. compilation error

e. runtime error

Correct answer: b.

When arrays are created their elements are initialized by default as follows:

Data Type	Default Value
boolean	false
byte	0
char	\u0000'
short	0
int	0
long	0L
float	0.0f
double	0.0d

String	null
Object	null

The elements of arr are of type Integer. Integer is a wrapper class, therefore the elements of the array are objects. According to the table above, they are initialized by default with null.

Q&A 126) What is the output of the following program? Select one correct answer.

```
class MyClass {
        public static void main(String[] args){
            int count = 1;
            for (int i = 0; i<10; i++) {
again:
            for (int j = 0; j<10; j++)
            if (i == j)
                 break again;
            count++;
            }
            System.out.println(count);
        }
}
```

a. compilation error

b. 10

c. 11

d. 46

e. 45

Correct answer: c.

Despite the indentation, the statement "count++" actually belongs to the outer for loop. The value of "count" will be incremented each time the outer loop is executed (10 times). Considering that the initial value of "count" is 1, then the final value will be 11.

Q&A 127) Which of the following are not Java keywords? Choose all that apply.

a. volatile

b. transient

c. goto

d. friend

e. import

f. include

g. expand

h. this

i. native

Correct answer: d, f, g.

Q&A 128) Which statements are true regarding the following Java class? Select one correct answer.

```
class MyClass {
    private static int data = 0;

    private void incrementData() {
        data++;                              // 1
    }
    private void decrementData() {
        data--;                              // 2
    }
    public static void doOperation(boolean
increment) {
        if (increment == true)
            incrementData();                 // 3
        else
            decrementData();                 // 4
    }
    public static void main(String[] args)
    {
        MyClass obj = new MyClass();
        obj.doOperation(true);               // 5
    }
}
```

a. compilation errors at //1 and //2 as non-static methods cannot access static members of a class

b. compilation errors at //3 and //4 as static methods cannot access non-static members of a class

c. compilation error at //5 a static method cannot be accessed using a reference variable

d. none of the above

Correct answer: b.

a. is incorrect as non-static methods can access static members of a class.

b. is correct, neither static variables nor static methods cannot access non-static variables and non-static methods of a class.

c. is in correct, a static variable can be accessed using an object reference variable or the name of the class.

d. is also incorrect.

Q&A 129) What will be the output of the following program? Select one correct answer.

```
class Base {
}
class Derived1 extends Base {
     void Method() {
    System.out.println("Method1");
     }
}
class Derived2 extends Base {
     void Method() {
         System.out.println("Method2");
     }
     public static void main(String[] args) {
         Derived1 d1 = new Derived1();
         Derived2 d2 = new Derived2();
         d1 = (Derived1)d2;              // 1
         d1.Method();
```

```
        }
}
```

a. compilation error at line // 1

b. it will throw `java.lang.ClassCastException`

c. it will display "`Method1`"

d. it will display "`Method2`"

Correct answer: a.

When trying to cast two unrelated classes, the code will fail to compile. Even if `Derived1` and `Derived2` have the same parent, there is no relationship between them.

Q&A 130) Which of the following implement checked exceptions? Choose all that apply.

```
a. class A extends RuntimeException

b. class A extends Throwable

c. class A extends Exception

d. class A extends IOException
```

Correct answer: c, d.

The base class for all type of exceptions is

253

```
java.lang.Throwable.
```

`java.lang.Error` **and** `java.lang.Exception` **both inherit from** `java.lang.Throwable`.

`java.lang.RuntimeException` **is a subclass of** `java.lang.Exception`.

Based on this class hierarchy exceptions can be divided into three main categories:

1. **Checked exceptions** – a checked exception is a subclass o f `java.lang.Exception`, **but not a subclass of** `java.lang.RuntimeException`

2. **Unchecked exceptions** (runtime exceptions) – a runtime exception is a subclass of `java.lang.RuntimeException`

3. **Errors** – an error is a subclass of `java.lang.Error`

Given these:

a. - is incorrect as class A is a subclass of `java.lang.RuntimeException` therefore an object of type A is a runtime exception.

b. - is incorrect as not all subclasses of `java.lang.Throwable` are checked exceptions.

c. and d. - are correct based on the definition of checked exceptions. (see 1. above)

Q&A 131) What is the output of the following code? Select one correct option:

```
public class MyClass {
    public static void main(String args[]) {
        int i = 10;
        {
            i++;
            System.out.println(i);
        }
        {

            i= i-1;
            System.out.println(i);
        }
    }
}
```

a. compilation error due to erroneous use of the brackets "{", "}" in the code

b. 10 10

c. 11 10

d. 10 9

e. 11 9

Correct answer: c.

Although it is not common practice, using braces to create two different blocks as in the example above, is allowed by the compiler.

Q&A 132) What is the output of the following program? Select one correct answer.

```
public class MyClass {
    public static void main(String[] args) {
        String s = "hello";
        s = new
StringBuilder(s).append(s).reverse().substring(0
, 4);
        System.out.println(s);
    }
}
```

a. hello

b. olle

c. olleh

d. olleho

e. compilation error

Correct answer: b.

The expression:

```
s = new
StringBuilder(s).append(s).reverse().substring(0
, 4);
```

is syntactically correct. The methods called in the expression can be chained, as append and reverse return a StringBuilder object and substring returns a String object.

The expression new
StringBuilder(s).append(s).reverse().substring(0

, 4) is evaluated from left to right as follows:

- new `StringBuilder(s)` will create a `StringBuilder` object with the content initialised to the content of the specified `String`, "hello"

- new `StringBuilder(s).append(s)` – appends hello to the existing character sequence. The new content becomes "hellohello"

- new `StringBuilder(s).append(s).reverse()` - the content becomes "olleholleh"

- new `StringBuilder(s).append(s).reverse().substring(0, 4)`

The `String` object generated is "olle".

Q&A 133) What types can be used in the "switch" statement's expression? Choose all that apply.

a. `byte, float, char`

b. `int, enum, short`

c. `String, char, byte`

d. `double, char, int`

e. `boolean, int, byte`

Correct answer: b, c.

switch **works with byte, short, char, int, enum and** String. **It also works with a few special classes that wrap certain primitive types:** Character, Byte, Short **and** Integer.

Q&A 134) What is the output of the following Java program? Select one correct answer.

```
import java.util.ArrayList;
import java.util.List;

public class MyClass {
    public static void main(String[] args) {
        List list = new ArrayList();          // 1
        list.add(0);
        list.add("one");                       // 2
        list.add(1, new Float(0.1));
        list.add(5);
        list.remove(3);                        // 3
        System.out.println(list);
    }
}
```

a. error at // 1 because element type is not specified

b. error at // 2 because we attempt to add a String in the same array list that already contains an integer

c. error at // 3 because "remove" is not a method of List Interface

d. it will print [0, 0.1, one]

e. it will print [0, 0.1, one, 5]

Correct answer: d.

When the type of the elements is not specified (as in `List<String> list`), the list is "heterogeneous" - it can contain any type Java objects. Thus statement // 1 is valid as well as adding a String after an Integer as it is the case for line // 2.

The `List` interface has a method `remove(int index)` which will do exactly what it says: it will remove the element at position `index` in the list.

In this particular example list.remove(3) will remove the element at position 3 in the list. As the element at position 3 is 5, the remaining elements in the list after the execution of line 3 are: 0, 0.1, one.

Q&A 135) Which of the following statements are true regarding "`break`" and "`goto`" statements in Java? Choose all that apply.

a. there is no difference between these two statements

b. there is no difference, but only when used inside loops

c. "`break`" can have both labeled and non labeled versions whereas "`goto`" can only have labeled version

d. "`break`" used outside a loop causes compilation error

e. "`goto`" is a reserved Java keyword but not currently used

Correct answer: d, e.

goto is a reserved keyword, but not currently used in Java.

Hence we cannot make any assumption on how it works in context of a. ,b. and c. above.

Also using `break` outside a loop causes a compilation error. So e. is also true.

Q&A 136) What class cannot be instantiated? Select all that apply.

a. an abstract class

b. a class with at least one abstract method

c. a class with static methods only

d. a class that implements an interface

Correct answers: a, b.

An abstract class cannot be instantiated, such attempt will cause compiler error.

A class that contains one or more abstract methods is an abstract class.

Therefore, answers a. and b. are correct.

Q&A 137) What is the output of the following program? Select one correct answer.

```
class Base {
    Base() {
```

```
        System.out.println("Constructor Base");
    }
    void Method() {
        System.out.println("Method Base");
    }
}
class Derived extends Base {
    Derived() {
        System.out.println("Constructor
Derived");
    }
    void Method() {
        System.out.println("Method Derived");
    }
}
class MyClass  {
    public static void main(String[] args) {
        Derived d = new Derived();
        d.Method();
    }
}
```

a.
```
Constructor Derived
Method Derived
```

b.
```
Constructor Base
Constructor Derived
Method Derived
```

c.
```
Constructor Base
Constructor Derived
MethodBase
Method Derived
```

d.

```
Constructor Derived
Constructor Base
MethodBase
Method Derived
```

Correct answer: b.

The general rule is: if a subclass constructor does not explicitly invoke a superclass constructor, the compiler automatically inserts a call to the no-argument constructor of the superclass.

Therefore, the construct: `Derived d = new Derived();` will first cause the Base class constructor to be called and then the Derived class constructor.

The statement `d.Method()` will call Method() defined in Derived class only.

Q&A 138) Given the following statements, select the correct options.

a. a `try` block can define multiple `finally` blocks

b. a `try` block can be followed by multiple `catch` blocks

c. both Error and checked exceptions need to be part of a method signature

d. `NullPointerException` is a thrown by the JVM when trying to access a method or a variable with a null value

Correct answer: a, d.

A `try` block cannot define multiple `finally` blocks but, can be followed by multiple `catch` blocks.

Checked exceptions need to be part of a method signature, but the same rule does not apply for Errors.

`NullPointerException` is a runtime exception thrown by the JVM as described above.

Q&A 139) What is the output of the following program?

```
public class MyClass {
    public static void main(String args[]) {
        int i = 1, j = 2;
        int r = i++ + 1 + 2*j;
        System.out.println(r);
    }
}
```

a. compilation error

b. 0

c. 3

d. 4

e. 5

f. 6

Correct answer: f.

Based on the operators precedence, the expression `r = i++ + 1 + 2*j` is evaluated as follows:

`r = 1 + 1 + 2*2`

`r = 6`

As the ++ operator is in postfix notation, i is incremented after the evaluation of the expression.

Q&A 140) What is the output of the following code? Select one correct answer:

```
String month = "Dec";
switch(month){
   case "Dec":
   case "Jan":
   case "Feb": System.out.println("Winter
months");
   case null: System.out.println("Other...");
}
```

a. it will print nothing

b. it will print `Winter months`

c. it will print `Other`

d. the code won't compile

Correct answer: d

The code will fail to compile as `null` is not allowed as a `case` label.